I

A Couple's Journey to a

THEE

Godly Marriage

WED

Live in Peace,
God bless
you!

Billy
+
Yolanda

I

A Couple's Journey to a

THEE

Godly Marriage

WED

BILLY & YOLANDA JACKSON

LIVE IN PEACE PUBLISHING

NASHVILLE

Manufactured in the United States of America
Interior Design by: Emma Primavera
Cover Design by: Liz Demeter

ISBN: 978-0-692-85962-9

Dedication

To our children Michele (Lakeem) Boyd, Alysa Jackson, Kennedy Martin, and William Jackson, Jr.:

May you experience the fullness of God and live out His plan and purpose for your lives, understanding that this will only be achieved by surrendering your lives totally unto Him.

To our grandchildren Angelique, Lakeem Jr., and Eris:

May you grow into Godly men and women, and in all your ways honor, acknowledge, and bring glory to God by what you say and do. In doing so, God will direct your path.

Love Always

Table of Contents

Acknowledgments

We first thank our Father, for through Him our salvation has come because of the sacrifice of His Son Jesus. With God all things are possible. Thank you, God, for allowing us, with the wisdom of Your Word and the endurance of past trials, to become the vessels and bearers of hope for others in the name of Jesus Christ. We are forever grateful for your love!

To our parents, Pastor William R. Harris, Sr., Susie A. Harris, Liletta M. Ward, Daniel D. Ward, and the late William I. Jackson: thank you for your love and life lessons. You have raised us in this world of chaos and struggle. Though times were tough on you, (times that we never saw), you continued to teach, guide, and prepare us for what life would throw at us. We are the fruits of your love and labor. When others see us as a couple, they see you and what God has allowed to grow in us through you. Thanks for being a Godly example on our journey.

To our children, Michele, (Lakeem, Sr.), Alysa, Kennedy, and William, Jr.: we pray that the testimony God has allowed us to record in these pages will serve as a guide for you and that it will help shape you into the person God created you to be.

To Pastor Vincent L. Windrow of Olive Branch Church, Nashville, Tennessee: we thank you for your guidance, direction, and inspiration. Thank you for having the vision of the vow and giving us the foundation for this book. May God continue to bless you, your family, and your ministry. May you continue to produce spiritual fruits so that by doing so others may come to know Jesus Christ our Lord and Savior.

Finally, to Mr. Mark Boone, our editor. Words cannot express the surgical operation you performed on our book. Your gentle and kind spirit encouraged us to keep pushing to create a piece of work that would transform lives. You helped us to capture those hard moments in our lives and escorted them into this book as lessons for life. We thank God for you, man of God, and appreciate your patience with us throughout this process.

Preface

Your wedding day! This is the day you've waited for. Even the hardest core man, who loves his man cave and night out with the boys, looks forward to the day he marries the woman of his dreams. You put on your tux, or whatever attire you've carefully chosen for the occasion. Your best man is right by your side, making sure that your tie is straight, your shoes are on the right feet, and you're sobered up from the previous night's final fling as a single man.

And what about you, the bride-to-be? You're putting on your beautiful wedding dress—the one designed specifically for you for this once-in-a-lifetime occasion. The dress that made the final cut out of hundreds of other dresses you have looked at and tried on. Your maid of honor is by your side, making sure that the stylist is on point, getting your hair perfect so that not a strand is out of place. Your mother is in the room, hovering about, examining the dress for any visible flaws or loose threads. All the while, you're going out of your mind, hoping everything will be perfect this day.

With all of this preparation, where is the thought about God's role in the impending union? You can be the best Christian on your good days, yet, on this one day, when you call on God, it's usually from a selfish motive, and often with the words: "Please God, let everyone get along and enjoy our wedding day!" or, "God, don't let anything unplanned happen!" or, "Lord, I hope he (or she) shows up, and on time and doesn't miss their cue!"

The purpose of the day and God's guiding hand in it is often forgotten, overlooked, or simply not considered at all. But truth be told, the meaning behind any vows exchanged without seeking God's blessing will be empty and will lack sustenance. It will exist only for the moment and will fail to serve as the foundation of a lasting relationship.

That is why we have been led to write this book. We don't want you to make the same mistakes and encounter the mishaps that we did when it comes to marriage. In this book, you will learn the story of our life together and how one misjudgment can lead to years of heartache and unnecessary pain.

This is not a traditional book on marriage about how, in a perfect world, your experience must be. It is the testimony of how we approached our vows in our first and second marriages and the hard lessons we learned. It's our testimony that we pray will help many couples who read it make good decisions led by their hearts and not their heads. If you believe in the power of God's miracles, then you have purchased the right book. Read and learn how God set us apart to be used for His glory. Understand how two broken people found God's saving power and peace through marriage. This transformational journey to a godly marriage saved us from ourselves and because He did it for us, we know that He can do the same for you.

We pray also that this book will be a guide for you to follow, whether you are contemplating marriage, engaged to be married, newly married, or have been married for several years. Therefore, when we write in the first person in this book, we are speaking to all who fall into each of these stages of the marital relationship.

You will find this book to be different from many that address marriage relationships and the central role that the wedding vow plays in the marriage ceremony. Each chapter alternates from the point of view of each partner in the relationship, providing the husband's and the wife's unique perspective through the lens of pain and suffering to deliverance and miracles in the relationship. It is a testimony of a second chance at marriage bestowed on us by the grace of God and strengthened by lessons we learned from earlier marriages that did not last. It is our intention that couples gain insight into marriage from a 360-degree perspective, and always with God at its center. We hope and pray that, after reading this book, you will have a clearer understanding of the importance of the marriage vow and how it continues to operate in your marriage long after the words were exchanged on your wedding day.

Billy and Yolanda Jackson

I Thee Wed

Understanding the Importance of the Wedding Vow

My wife-to-be Yolanda and I stood together at the altar with stars in our eyes, knees knocking, holding each other's sweaty palms while the pastor began the ceremony. We were concentrating solely on each other and what we were getting ready to say. Earlier during our yearlong engagement, we decided to adapt the traditional vow to include our own heartfelt promise to one another expressed in our own words.

When these words were recited, you could hear the approvals of our family and friends who were in the audience with their "yeses" and "amens." This was confirmation for us, who were very nervous at the time. As the ceremony progressed to the obligatory "I do," the ringing declaration "and now I pronounce you husband and wife," and the final command "You may salute your bride," a loud cheer erupted from the audience. It was now official: We were Mr. and Mrs. Billy Jackson.

Remembering our wedding, I distinctly recall the vows we made to each other and being very thankful for our union, knowing that this time, the second time around for me, God had His hand in our marriage. I had many flaws. My lifestyle was not one that Yolanda would have been attracted to. However, I knew that differences between couples are not always deal breakers.

I remember the first time Yolanda had been to my house after we first met. I had invited her to dinner, unaware at the time of how the way I was living might be received by her. Thinking back, I had to have known that my living quarters were not the best. So I put things away, hid some of my junk, and prepared a wonderful meal. I just knew that the night was going to be right. I was excited that Yolanda was coming over to spend some time with me. In the back of my mind, however, I was still concerned about what she might think of me. As the saying goes, "First impressions are lasting impressions."

I had been living like that for a while, tolerating the disorder, and now I found myself furiously trying to clean up. That was the beginning of many changes for me, and I barely recognized it.

When she arrived, I knew that although I had tried my best to present a pleasing environment for her, I could tell I had fallen short. The words out of her mouth were tactful and well intentioned, but her face revealed her obvious disgust.

Escorting her to the bathroom so that she could wash her hands for the dinner I had prepared, it dawned on me that I had not put out any hand towels for her to dry them. All my towels and hand cloths were in the dirty clothes, which were piled high in the same closet that I had just opened to retrieve a clean one for her. The only clean towels I had were ones I'd never used. I offered one of those to her, but she objected and finally said with a smile, "Air drying works just as well."

Looking back on that day, and knowing my wife as I do now, it was nothing but God's will and His good grace that kept her interested in a relationship that I thought was destined to self-destruct.

I believed God's will and intent for the success of our marriage would be a strength I would need because I wasn't confident about the kind of person I was then for my future wife. I asked myself the question: "Could I be the man she thought I was?" The promise I made during the ceremony to be that man was not made in confidence because I still didn't understand the importance of the vow.

The Meaning of the Word "Vow"

We hear the word "vow" so often that we lose focus on its meaning and how it pertains to us as married couples. The word "vow" means a solemn promise, pledge, or commitment to another.

In scripture, Moses sets forth the rules about vows by speaking to the leaders of the tribes in these words:

> *Then Moses summoned the leaders of the tribes of Israel and told them, "This is what the LORD has commanded: A man who makes a vow to the LORD or makes a pledge under oath must never break it. He must do exactly what he said he would do.*
>
> *— NUMBERS 30: 1–2*

When we enter into a relationship in which we promise one another that we will be with him or her forever, the words "promise," "pledge," and "commitment" must not just be mouthed; they must permeate us, meaning they should be a part of our very being. They should be as seeds planted in our hearts, which grow into a life that embodies our union as husband and wife, a union that continually remembers, embraces, and honors the vows made to each other on the wedding day. This is expressed beautifully in ECCLESIASTES 5: 4–5:

> When you make a promise to God, don't delay in following through, for God takes no pleasure in fools. Keep all the promises you make to him. It is better to say nothing than to make a promise and not keep it.

What the Vow Represents

After years of being married, I have learned the true value of the marriage vow. Think about for a moment, the lessons we learn when we are young. When I was growing up and living with my parents, they gave me assigned chores, such as taking out the trash, keeping my room clean, and keeping my grades up. These assignments were confirmed with my acknowledgment and promise that those duties would be carried out. When I failed to do so, I failed to keep my promise, my "vow."

As children, we don't understand why our parents are upset when we fall short in carrying out these responsibilities, yet as adults, and as parents ourselves, we have come to learn the importance of the vow and try to teach that to our children. But as adults, even with the knowledge of the sanctity of the vow, we often fall short when it comes to carrying out the vows we make to each other on our wedding day.

In my previous marriage, I had fallen short in carrying out the marriage vow. I share this so that you may understand that getting married and making a vow to your loved one is a serious matter.

My journey in becoming a husband began when I became a father at the young age of twenty-one from a college relationship that was not intended for marriage. My first-born daughter entered the world in December of 1989. This relationship with my daughter's mother was not a serious one, and so, lacking a commitment to each other, we eventually broke up. Shortly afterwards, the total responsibility for taking care of my daughter weighed on my shoulders. I was now considered a single father with an infant daughter. Quickly, I had to figure out how to raise this beautiful little girl. Unfortunately, being a father and provider came first, so I was unable to finish college.

Operating as a single parent wore on me, and the job I had was not great. Almost a year after my daughter had been born an old girlfriend from college came back into my life. She immediately took on the mother role for my daughter. It was really easy for me to enjoy the comfort from the help I received being a single parent. At this time, I was also introduced to the military, as her father was an officer in the U.S. Navy. I believed then that I was in love and ready for marriage. As I look back, I realize that if I had not been a father living as a single parent, I would not have considered marriage at all. I wasn't saved and, therefore, God was not a part of any vow I made at that time.

In September 1990, my first wife and I were married. I couldn't have told you what salvation meant at the time, but in my mind, everything fit what I considered then to be a marriage. In my mind, I told myself: "This is the right thing to do. It's time for me to settle down. This is good; someone to help me raise my daughter." No other thought or consideration occurred to me when I decided to become a husband. No counseling, no outside advice on considering the pros and cons, and I definitely did not read books about marriage.

In February 1992, we bore a child together, and now I had two beautiful daughters. My back was against the wall, and I had to buckle down and make a decision on how I was going to provide for my family. I was a husband and father with no "real" job. I needed to get serious and decide on a career and life for my family. So, on April 1, 1993, I enlisted in the United States Army. It was my decision, and it took me away from the southeast: Tennessee and Alabama, the homes of my mother, father, and most of my relatives. I would be isolated with my wife and daughters away from all of my sources of comfort.

My commitment to the marriage remained solely on the basis of my duties as a parent. After the fourth year, the strain of arguments and alcohol began to weigh in on the marriage. Being in the service, I was away from home a lot, and it affected the longevity of the marriage. My wife and I could not see eye to eye, and I didn't care if my use of alcohol was becoming a factor in our relationship. There were no deep roots planted in this relationship, and I knew that deep down inside, it was a matter of time before the marriage would end because we didn't want to fight for it.

I remember a conversation about marriage that I had with my father during that time. He told me that he was by no means an expert in marital affairs since he had been divorced twice. But he did say that if there was love in it, I should try my best to work it out. If not, let it go. That conversation came back to me a couple of years later when he died of a massive heart attack while playing tennis. When I laid my father to rest, I realized that I could not continue on the journey in the marriage.

After several conversations with my wife, we decided to divorce. Although we had been married for thirteen years and I was now a single man again, in my heart being a husband was what I wanted in life. I wanted it, but I was prepared to live my life and grow old alone if the right person didn't come into my life. I was not going to hunt down the next Mrs. Jackson. In fact, I decided not to even look. Instead, I wanted to work on me and fix some of the personal problems I had that affected others. I wanted to make sure that I would be the right man for the right woman. For that, I knew I needed God's help to value the marriage vow.

When we recite our vows to each other in the presence of our Lord, not only are we making a commitment to that person, we are thanking God for His blessing over the union by committing to Him as well. We make that commitment in front of witnesses whom we love—our families and our friends. We are telling them, this is the one whom I will love and cherish for the rest of my life. This is the one to whom I will be loyal. To all on that day, we have become a light in the world that shows how two can become one. We represent the Guest of Honor, our Father in Heaven. This representation is God's living evidence of His existence in our lives and His anointing of the union taking place.

The "Glue" That Binds Us Together

As a result of my first experience in marriage, I have learned that the marriage vows are at the center of the wedding ceremony, and their exchange is the most anticipated part of the service. Although the two of you came to the ceremony as two separate individuals, you leave as one. The marriage vows are the glue that binds you together.

The wedding day is not "show time," for the words spoken during the ceremony will not only be remembered, but will articulate the intent and vision of the two who are joined in holy matrimony. Thus, they should be words that must be kept and held accountable to by the person who utters them.

The vow exchanged on your wedding day should outweigh any other commitment you make in your life, other than your commitment to follow Christ. Your desire to fulfill the marriage vow should be so strong that it becomes your first priority in the union.

At the beginning of a relationship, we often have no idea what God has intended for us. We may know that we love each other, or that we aspire to have the same things out of life, or that we want to live the rest of our lives with the one we love. It is our intent to be the best person we can be in the marriage, an intent codified by the vow we make to each other.

Once the intent is made clear, it must be followed by a promise, a commitment made to never give up on the marriage, no matter how tough the going may get. Just as life hits us hard as individuals, new trials unknown to us will come to us as a couple, but as written in ROMANS 12:12, we must:

> *Rejoice in our confident hope. Be patient in trouble, and keep on praying.*

Persevering in Marriage

Through our vows, we must pledge to one another to persevere no matter what comes our way. We must commit to being patient with each other because the trials you endure as a couple strengthen you to accept and enjoy future blessings. Thus, your vows must include the promise of trusting in the Lord when the untested waters of marriage are crossed.

The seeds planted by your vows must be continually watered and nourished to grow those deep and strong roots, roots deep enough to keep your marriage in place so that no matter how strong the wind, the marriage will remain intact and never founder. Then, after every storm, the both of you can enjoy the blessings of the fruits born from your endurance of those trials, and all of this because you've kept the promises you made to each other:

*They are like trees planted along a riverbank,
with roots that reach deep into the water.
Such trees are not bothered by the heat or
worried by long months of drought.
Their leaves stay green, and they never stop
producing fruit.*
— *JEREMIAH 17:8*

Questions for You to Reflect On

1. What words do you especially remember from your wedding vow?

2. How often do you reflect on the vow you made to your spouse?

3. If you could change the vows you made, how might you change them?

Respecting Our Differences and Aligning Our Values

When my husband Billy and I were dating, we spent a lot of time together unpacking our past, voicing our likes and dislikes, and embracing our personal truths. We soon came to realize that we had come from two different backgrounds and that we viewed life very differently.

Billy grew up with parents who had divorced, and I was raised with parents who had been married for more than forty years. He had two teenaged daughters from a previous relationship and marriage, and I had a daughter who was a toddler. I had been married for three years, and Billy had been married for thirteen years before our relationship—not to mention that he is eight years older than I.

Billy had already served seven years in the United States Army as an aircraft mechanic and was stationed in such faraway places as upstate New York, Hawaii, and, closer to home, Fort Campbell, Kentucky. I met him in his second career as a police officer for the city of Nashville, Tennessee.

At the time, I was in my first career, climbing the corporate ladder in the beauty and wellness business where I became the director of one of the largest spas in Middle Tennessee.

Insofar as our faith life was concerned, Billy would come to church and leave before the benediction was delivered, whereas I was raised by a pastor of the Baptist Church and attended Sunday school, staying at church most of the day. I can say that we had differences that were very visible. One may wonder how we made our relationship work.

All I knew was that my spirit kept confirming that Billy was the one, and that we would live our lives together forever. Yes, on the surface, there were many differences between us that could have ended the relationship. For instance, he desired to be married again, and I was uninterested in going through another marriage ceremony. Yet, I did value my relationship with God, my family, and the love Billy and I had for one another. I just didn't want the lifetime, hard-to-get-out-of commitment of marriage. You see, I had been let down before, and I didn't want to relive that experience.

We fell in love and began a relationship. Billy was working the night shift and raising his oldest teenage daughter alone, while his other daughter was living with her mom. He was struggling with taking care of her while working a full-time job, so I felt compelled to help him.

She began to stay with me during the week, and I would take her to school. The arrangement worked for us so well that Billy started staying over during the week also. We were becoming one family, dealing with the challenges of raising a teen and a toddler. Yet, we knew that "shacking up" meaning living together without the benefit of marriage, and fornicating was sinful, in addition to outside the will of God. It didn't really trouble me because getting married was a distant thought in my mind. After all, I had been there and done that!

After some thought, we decided to sell Billy's home and live under my roof. It was then that we realized we were not setting a good example for our children and that we needed to do what was right by God.

During this time, we worshipped God and served Him on the weekends, but kept Him at arm's length when it came to our personal behavior. Admittedly, that did not get us off to a good start. All along I knew that Billy valued the institution of marriage and family, and he continually expressed the desire to be married one day again. Even knowing that, I was still trapped by my feelings toward marriage. This was a recipe for a failed relationship, for as scripture says:

> *Can two people walk together*
> *without agreeing on the direction?*
> *— AMOS 3:3*

Aligning Our Values

I was hesitant about going into marriage with Billy solely because of fear. Fear had me bound to think: "What if he does the same thing as my last husband? What if it doesn't work out? What if I am pulled away from my family and friends again?"

All of these thoughts were coming from a place of fear. I had no faith in relationships during this time, so, I just kept moving along in a state of fear. I could not deal with the repercussions of two potentially failed marriages. So why bother?

This was so wrong on my part and not fair to the man whom I truly loved. I had to transform my mind to understand that the right thing to do would be to admit that it was only fear that caused these thoughts and feelings about marriage. I needed to honor God by submitting this fear to Him, and I had to deal with it by turning that fear into faith. By changing my mindset, I was able to say "yes" to Billy and marry him. Had I held onto my fears based on my past experiences and failures, God would not have been pleased, and I would have remained in bondage.

Going into our marriage, I knew that my husband-to-be valued God and his family. Those values were very attractive to me because I valued the same things. Understanding and agreeing to what your spouse values will set the foundation for your marriage, for only then will you both be on one accord. Once our values became aligned, I realized how important it was to me that I married a man who first seeks the Lord and had an active relationship with Jesus Christ. This requirement is essential when circumstances of life attempt to disrupt the union. According to scripture:

> *For a husband is the head of his wife as Christ is the head of the church. He is the Savior of his body, the church.*
> — *EPHESIANS 5:23*

Scripture also says that you must beware of outside forces that seek to harm your marriage. In the words of 1 PETER 5:8:

Two

…Watch out for your great enemy, the devil.
He prowls around like a roaring lion, looking
for someone to devour.

The enemy is looking to attack the head. If the head is attacked, then the wife and children will be under attack. Thus, husbands must have the wisdom and knowledge to combat the enemy to protect their family. This injunction is at the core of Christian marriage. Without it, it is nearly impossible for a marriage to succeed. A wife will not win if she believes that money and other superficial attributes will bail her out of the enemy's attacks.

Knowing that despite the troubles that may come, being blessed with the knowledge that Billy and I now have our faith to rely on is comforting to me. Our shared values have got us through. To determine what your spouse values, ask yourself:

- What are your spouse's personal goals, dreams, and aspirations?

- What are your family's common goals?

- How do your spouse's values fit within the family's common goals?

- What does success mean to the family?

- How can you help your family succeed?

- What are your limits to what you are willing to do?

Answering these questions with your spouse or spouse-to-be will help to shed light on where your marriage is heading and will identify whether you are on the same page. Before you exchange your vows, take the time to understand your spouse's values. Doing so will help to establish your relationship on a firm foundation. Consider these words from scripture:

> *But don't begin until you count the cost. For who would begin construction of a building without first calculating the cost to see if there is enough money to finish it? Otherwise, you might complete only the foundation before running out of money, and then everyone would laugh at you. They would say, "There's the person who started that building and couldn't afford to finish it!"*
> — *Luke 14:28–30*

Jesus is teaching the disciples the importance of counting up the cost of being a disciple. You may ask: What does this have to do with marriage and vows?

The Goal of a Godly Marriage

The goal of a Godly marriage is to be Christ's disciples and to glorify God in everything you do. This means that you can't love your spouse more than you love Jesus, your kids and parents more than Jesus, and your reputation or your economic security more than Jesus. Your foundation must be Jesus Christ, which is all you need to build your marriage on.

In order for your values to be aligned with your spouse's so that you can envision what God has for your marriage, you must eliminate selfishness from your life completely. Even in the small things. For instance, one person should not be the one who exclusively determines where to eat. Consider your spouse's palate and where he or she desires to eat. When you don't consider your spouse's interests, it will be impossible to submit to your husband as unto the Lord.

Some ways by which you can achieve this are by lifting each other up in times of trial, seeking to understand one another better, and by capitalizing on each other's differences rather than dwelling on them as negatives.

Because no two people are alike, there will inevitably be times that become so trying that, you may put each other down when trying to cope in married life. But as a married couple, joined together in love and in Christ, you must lift each other up. Invariably, one of the two in a marriage is the stronger of the two. That person must be cognizant of this and must boost the other when it becomes necessary. By stepping up to raise up his or her spouse, that partner is fulfilling God's will for the marriage.

We demonstrate understanding of one another when we offer constructive criticism designed to build up our spouse, sharing our wisdom with love. God's plan for us as a couple starts with us as individuals. We have lived most of our lives moving in our own self-centered circles, picking up selfish habits along the way that become part of our character. These habits get in the way of living for others instead of ourselves. Often, through our spouses, God gives us direction for shedding these bad habits. Men, all too frequently, do not want to hear this from their wives, taking the worldly view rather than forsaking it for the spiritual. God is telling you: "I need you to respond this way. I've provided your wife to help me in this endeavor."

God's blessing of your union will bear the fruit of many blessings. Of course, along with these blessings come responsibilities. Because you are no longer individuals, the task God gives you must be completed together. This means that there are complementary strengths that you each have; that is, what one lacks, the other has. Men must learn humility and must follow their wife's lead when God calls her to show us them the way.

Capitalizing on Our Differences

One interest that my husband Billy had that I didn't share was riding motorcycles. Ironically, my father and my brother loved motorcycles and both had one. One day, when we were dating, Billy rode up to my house on a brand-new Suzuki Boulevard C50 motorcycle. He knew full well that my feelings about motorcycles were shaped by my father's having had an accident on one and my younger cousin's dying in a motorcycle accident. So why did he think that I was going to approve? After a heated debate, I lost the battle, and Billy ended up keeping this motorcycle.

Eventually, I conceded that motorcycle riding is a hobby that my husband and family members enjoy. One day, when we were having dinner at my parents, I announced that I planned to take the motorcycle course to get a license. Billy looked at me and asked, "Are you serious?" I replied that I was. Was he excited! Within a couple of weeks, I was a licensed motorcyclist.

Because I knew the passion that he had for riding his motorcycle would not go away, I had to consider my husband's interests. By setting my past feelings aside and through prayer, I was able to eliminate a source of tension and thus put to rest this contentious aspect of our marriage. After I got my license, I bought my own motorcycle, and we traveled many back roads together—even making family trips to Florida and Alabama. As an added benefit, it enabled us to spend quality time together that otherwise we would have missed had I remained inflexible.

Questions for You to Reflect On

1. Do you believe that your personal differences affect your relationship? If so, how?

2. How can you capitalize more on your differences in your relationship?

3. In what ways have your values helped you through life's challenges to your relationship?

4. In what area of your relationship do you remain inflexible? What might you do to overcome the inflexibility?

Being Convicted by the Holy Spirit

It was November 7, 2004, and at that time, I had made a habit of being at church thirty minutes early. I wanted to make sure I got a seat before service started. Our church had two sections for seating—the main sanctuary in front of the pulpit and to the left of it, the "overflow" side, where a large screen was installed so that the pulpit, which was otherwise blocked, could be projected for all on that side to see.

I sat in the main sanctuary on the left side, eight rows back in the seat right next to the wall. Up until that day I had been looking at Yolanda from afar as she sat on the right side with her mother and daughter. On that day, I decided to act. Several weeks before, I had nervously walked into the office of the pastor (who happened to be Yolanda's father) and said: "Pastor, I have a question for you. If you say 'no,' I will never bring it up again, but would you mind if I take your daughter out for lunch or an early dinner?"

I nervously awaited his response. He smiled as he looked down at his desk and replied, "Good luck to you, son. At this time in her life, she is mad at all men."

Three

With a sigh of relief, I took it as his blessing and I proceeded with my plan. In my mind, Yolanda's being mad at all men was merely a formality.

On that day in November I waited for her to enter the sanctuary before service began. When she looked in my direction, I motioned for her to meet me half way, at the end of my pew. I extended my hand, and she responded. As we shook hands and exchanged pleasantries, I pulled a piece of paper out of my pocket that had my phone number on it and handed it to her. She looked at it without reaching for it, as if I were handing her something dirty. "If you wouldn't mind, could you call me? I thought maybe we could go out to dinner," I said.

I remember it as clearly as if it happened yesterday. After hesitating for about ten seconds, she mouthed the word, "Sure." She took the slip of paper and walked back to join her mother.

She called me on the ninth of November, and the following weekend we went out to eat. On that date I was nervous because there was something about Yolanda. I just felt it in my spirit. We decided that we would meet for dinner and a movie. I stood by the entrance waiting for her to arrive. When she did, it was like she was walking toward me in slow motion. She had on a black sweater with a necklace and jeans. Her hair was beautiful and flawless. She had on glasses that complemented her smile. Thinking back on that night, I was witnessing the wonderful blessing that had come into my life as I stood there waiting to greet her. The evening went so well that we began dating shortly afterward. Spending time together was great! The time soon came when I knew the relationship was getting serious.

Every Thanksgiving I would go to Alabama and spend the holiday with my mother and sisters. I would take off work, leave Nashville on the Wednesday before the holiday, and stay through Sunday. I rarely missed, and I never cut that weekend short.

On that one trip after meeting Yolanda, I talked to her on the phone on most of the drive down. We talked when I got there and before I went to bed. Thanksgiving Day I did the normal holiday fellowship, but I missed her terribly. She wouldn't admit it, but I could tell that she missed me too. "Do you have to stay down there the whole time?" she had asked. "You said Sunday is when you are coming back, right?"

That Friday morning, I got up and told my mother that I had to get back to Nashville. She smiled at me and I knew what she was thinking. Before she could say anything, I said, "Yep, this may be the one." I drove back to Nashville.

I remember thinking the whole trip back home, "What can I get her to show her how much I miss her?" I was a divorcé with my own home, and I was prepared to open my life, my time, and my privacy to her. I had nothing to hide, so I was going to give her a set of keys to my house. I thought it was a good idea at the time.

When I arrived in Nashville, I went straight to see her. It was apparent to me that she was just as excited to see me as I was to see her. We embraced with a kiss. Then we sat down on the couch and began to talk. When I saw an opening in the conversation, I put a set of my house keys on her coffee table for her to see. She asked me what they were, and when I told her, she was taken aback. In all of my excitement, I never thought about how fast I was going. It hadn't been a month since I had given her my number, and yet I was giving her the keys to my house. Giving her the keys to my home to me was like giving her the keys to my heart. Nevertheless, I realized then that even though it was done with good intentions, it may have been a little too fast.

We continued to spend time together. A month after the day I gave her my phone number, I told her that I loved her; it was December 7, 2004. I knew she was the one.

There was no doubt in my mind that it was Yolanda whom I wanted the honor of marrying. I was not the man I was supposed to be in my first marriage. But this one would be, had to be, different, I vowed. I wasn't marrying her because the good things about us outweighed the bad. No. I was marrying Yolanda because it was easy for me to love her—who she was as a woman—and I was excited about who we could become together.

I didn't have anyone to tell me what to expect, or how to prepare to be the man I should be to lay a strong foundation for a fruitful marriage. What I did have were the experiences of a failed first marriage and the knowledge of what doesn't work to build a strong one. I still had a long way to go, but there was no doubt in my heart about the commitment that I was prepared to make for this marriage journey.

I did not write out my vows because I knew in my heart why I was marrying Yolanda. I know now that I was not the man God wanted me to be then, but I thank Him every day for the time He gave me with her before we were married. It was during that time we spent together that God gave me the wisdom to comprehend the woman that she was. As I stood before her in front of God and all the witnesses, God put these words in my heart on our wedding day:

> One of the most precious gifts that God has ever blessed me with was you. I love you. And I love you not just because you are a great woman, a great mother, a great teacher, and friend. I love you because you make it so easy to love you. I promise to be there through trials and tribulations. I'll always have your hand. Whenever tragedy strikes, when you look up from crying I'll be right there. I love you.... thank you for this.

I look back on the vow I made and I see truth in it. When I spoke of falling in love and being excited about a future together, that was the truth as I felt it. When I told my wife that she was one of God's most precious gifts to me, that, too, was the truth. And when I told her that I fell in love with her because she made it so easy to love her, I meant it with all my heart.

During the time that I was not living a righteous life, I was still fighting my addiction to alcohol, which found a stronghold in my life. But God still blessed me with Yolanda despite how I was living. He knew that one day I would be saved and would surrender to His will, and I eventually received my salvation. Because of His grace and mercy, what I vowed on that day, our wedding day, became the truth of my sanctification. The truth that God taught me by blessing me with a second chance can be summed up in these words of scripture:

> *Do not love this world nor the things it offers you, for when you love the world, you do not have the love of the Father in you. For the world offers only a craving for physical pleasure, a craving for everything we see, and pride in our achievements and possessions. These are not from the Father, but are from this world.*
> — *1 JOHN 2:15–16*

I am a different person now than I was then, and I mean every word today as strongly as I spoke them in 2007. I believe that the Holy Spirit was interceding on my behalf before I realized what I had found in Yolanda. As much as we have come through by the grace and mercy of God in heaven, there is no way I could have envisioned where we are today:

> *When the Spirit of truth comes, he will guide you into all truth. He will not speak on his own but will tell you what he has heard. He will tell you about the future. He will bring me glory by telling you whatever he receives from me. All that belongs to the Father is mine; this is why I said, "The Spirit will tell you whatever he receives from me."*
> — *JOHN 16:13–15*

Questions for You to Reflect On

1. Did you have any doubts about marrying your spouse? If so, what were they?

2. What made you overcome those doubts?

3. What bad habits have you brought into your relationship? What have you done to try to overcome them?

4. How has marrying your spouse made you a different person that you were before you married him or her?

Four

The Meaning of the Marriage Covenant

A covenant is a formal, solemn, and binding agreement, a written pact or promise usually under seal between two or more parties, especially for the performance of some action. It comes from the Latin word *convenīre*, meaning "to come together, agree." When I think of the word covenant, I immediately reflect on the Old Testament and the covenant God made to Abraham:

> *The LORD had said to Abram, "Leave your native country, your relatives, and your father's family, and go to the land that I will show you. I will make you into a great nation. I will bless you and make you famous, and you will be a blessing to others. I will bless those who bless you and curse those who treat you with contempt. All the families on earth will be blessed through you.*
> *— GENESIS 12:1–3*

I Thee Wed

In this scripture, God told Abraham to "Go to the land that I will show you." In this verse, Abraham had to do something. What he had to do, he had no clue about how it would turn out; however, he was obedient to God's call. Abraham and his wife Sarah had to leave to follow God's command. God promised to make Abraham's name great and to make him the father of many nations. He said, "I will take care of those who trouble you and the families that come after you will be blessed because they come from your bloodline." This was a big promise from God, but we can't miss the key point here, which is that it was Abraham's obedience and sacrifice that resulted in God's blessings on him and his family. God trusted Abraham enough to say, "You are the one I will bless." Why would God say such a thing if He really didn't mean it? A promise this amazing would need careful consideration.

In holy matrimony, husband and wife vow to stay together through sickness and health and until death do them part. Through the good times and bad times. In marriage, you are making a covenant unto God. A covenant that is final and irrevocable. This is totally different from the worldly promises we make on a day-to-day basis, promises that we forget were made and do not think about again until the week has passed. We cannot go into marriage with the same mindset.

At times we treat the wedding vows the same way we treat any other promise we make. We stand at the altar with the officiant facing us and a throng of people behind us and recite empty words that have little or no meaning for us. After the ceremony is over, many married couples do not even remember what they said or promised at the altar.

We must stop pretending. We must stop mouthing words that are empty of meaning. Either we are going to vow to stick and stay, or not make a vow at all. Either we are in this commitment together, or we don't commit at all.

I learned this the hard way. I realized that I did it all wrong when I married the first time, thinking that it would solve and heal my internal problems, not thinking at all about the promise I was making to and before God.

When you marry, you need the knowledge, wisdom, and faith to keep your commitment to God and to your spouse. For God has kept His promise. He has blessed our name, our nation, and children for generations. What we fail to realize is that we must believe in God and uphold the covenant with Him just as Abraham did. We must know that God fights our battles and that we are not fighting a war that has not been won. This war has been won through the blood of Jesus Christ. The enemy has been defeated, and Jesus is our victorious Lord and Savior.

When a Covenant Becomes a Contract in Marriage

A contract is a binding agreement between two or more persons or parties—especially one that is legally enforceable. A contract has a starting and an ending date. It is a document produced by one party which the other party accepts. It serves as a reminder for what each person has agreed upon. It is created because one is not sure that he or she will reap the benefits promised.

When you approach marriage with the mentality that it constitutes a contract, you are entering into dangerous territory. Marriage is not a contract; it is a covenant. When people ask: "Why should I get married?" or say, "We have the benefits of being married; we live together, and we even have children together." or "What's the point of signing a piece of paper? After so many years, we are considered married anyway under the 'common law,' right?" Such statements are coming from a mindset of marriage being a contract. In many instances, it is not raised to the level of a covenant as it should be.

As my relationship with Billy started to progress, and marriage began to be the topic of discussion, I told him that I didn't want to marry again whenever he would bring it up in conversation. I would give the impression that marriage was not important to me. I would respond by saying, "Why should we get married? We're good; we don't need that piece of paper to say 'I love you' and that 'I am here for you.'" Sound familiar?

Truth be told, I was fearful and could not muster up the courage to go through another marriage ceremony. Getting another dress, inviting people, determining a date—it was all so unnecessary to me. These feelings were real, but what I discovered is that they were really a disguise for my fear. Fear of failing at marriage a second time around. Fear of facing others and their opinions about my decision. Fear of wondering who will support this marriage, when my last one didn't work. I had to stop and take full responsibility and admit that it was my actual fears that held me back from moving forward. It was my lack of trust in God. I didn't respect or value the covenant with God, which is the whole point of marriage. I truly loved the concept, the idea of being married, but could not overcome my fears.

In my case, I, too, viewed marriage as a contract rather than as a covenant. Contracts can be rendered null and void at any time, and in most cases, the parties don't even have hard feelings toward each other if the marriage doesn't work out—the so-called "irreconcilable differences" divorce. The belief prevails that if the marriage works, great; if it doesn't, oh well; at least I tried. So why spend the money and go through the "hoopla" of it all. Boy, was I wrong and in need to repent from this mindset!

In reality, the contractual marriage is a cop-out for not acknowledging God's role in ordaining your marriage. If God is not the foundation of your life, you will find yourself viewing the marriage covenant as just another legal bind. The excuses that you make contribute to a lack of trust and to your distance from God. If, as an unmarried person, your relationship with God is lacking, then it is going be difficult for you to view marriage as a covenant. You will always have the perspective that it is just a contract.

It doesn't matter if you have been a churchgoer all your life. The question remains, what is your relationship with God? What do you believe is God's view about the marriage covenant? We either stand on the promises of God, or we don't. The bible teaches us:

Just say a simple, 'Yes, I will,' or 'No, I won't.'
Anything beyond this is from the evil one.
— MATTHEW 5:37

So where do you stand on the view of marriage as being based on a covenant versus being based on a contract? Now that you know your "yes" should be yes and your "no" should be no, how strongly are you or will you be committed to the vows exchanged on your wedding day?

What you say to your spouse is not just a performance for all who come to witness your wedding. The very words that you express to your spouse are being uttered as a promise, as a covenant with and before God. This means that your words should come from your heart and should seal the blessing that God will anoint on the both of you and your marriage. This blessing is not only for the joy you will receive during this journey, but also for the motivation, the healing, and the strength you both will need to endure the trials you will face together.

Marriage Is a Covenant before God

In marriage, we must be truthful to the vow and read the fine print, knowing that it is a covenant before God. The covenant is made first to God, then to our spouse, and lastly to the witnesses. In the Old Testament we find more intense practices when a covenant was made with God for people. These practices included killing and butchering of an animal, which was considered to bind the covenant. In God's covenant with Abram—soon to be Abraham—for instance, God had very specific instructions for the animals Abram was to bring forth, and he was to cut them in half. This is considered a sacrifice before the Lord. While we don't adhere to this ritual today, our pledging our lives to another before God represents another form of sacrifice.

We must keep this in mind when we are preparing to make a covenant before God.

Here are four steps you can take for a successful Christian marriage as you prepare to take your vows. They apply to the wedding or to renewing your vows, whether you choose to write your own or recite those upheld by Christian tradition.

Step 1: Read the covenants found in the bible. This will give you the knowledge and strength to make a promise before God. It will also deepen your personal commitments:

- The Covenant of Adam: GENESIS 1:26–30, GENESIS 2:16–17, and GENESIS 3:15–19

- The Covenant of Noah: GENESIS 9

- The Convent of Abraham: GENESIS 12:1–7, GENESIS 15, and GENESIS 22:15–18

- The Covenant of Palestine: DEUTERONOMY 30:1–10

- The Covenant of David: 2 SAMUEL 7:8–16

- The New Covenant: JEREMIAH 31:31–34, MATTHEW 5:17, EPHESIANS 2:8–9

Step 2: Set aside time to write down what you are praying and believing in God for in your marriage as well as what you believe to be true about your spouse. This is important because you are setting the course for your marriage journey. Your coming together as one will take on many transformations. As you are becoming who God is calling you to be, the enemy will throw in its stresses and worries. When both of you have already established what you believe in God for your marriage that He has blessed, His Word will be your defense for all the attempts to disqualify, defeat, and destroy your growth as a couple. The enemy will be on the job, attempting to divide and conquer. He will not gain a foothold in your marriage if you follow this step together.

Step 3: Share with your fiancé, fiancée, husband, or wife what you believe in your heart to be true regarding your marriage covenant. Be sure you are listening actively to each other. Do not jump to conclusions or persuade your spouse-to-be of your beliefs.

Step 4: Together record the ways in which you will adhere to your marriage covenant until death do you part, so that when the day comes for you to declare them aloud on your wedding day, you express them with conviction and love. As written in JAMES 4:17:

> *Remember, it is sin to know what you ought to do and then not do it.*

The Marriage Covenant Requires Sacrifice

Today, you don't normally hear "I am in covenant with my spouse." While this expression may not be commonly used in the twenty-first century, we must always remember it in the context of our marriage and that it is to be upheld. Just think about it for a moment. Had it not been for God who made the covenant with Abraham, we would not be a blessed people. In fact, the only reason we are free today is because of the covenant that God had with Jesus Christ, and Jesus Christ held true to this covenant. So why are we so quick to break the marriage covenant? Why do we not fight for it when marriage becomes inconvenient for us?

The reason is that we lack a sense of sacrifice. We don't want to sacrifice anything for another. If there is nothing in it for us, we're quick to quit or give up. We must discard this selfish perspective about marriage. Marriage takes sacrifice! It is unhealthy and will continue to be destructive to the union of a husband and a wife if he or she is not willing to make the necessary sacrifices for the good of each other.

The way we can see this more clearly in marriage is when we walk down the aisle to the altar, the structure that was built when an offering or sacrifice was to be made unto God. In GENESIS 8:20 as Noah was leaving the Ark, he built an altar and sacrificed some of the clean animals and birds unto the Lord. It was when the Lord noticed this sacrifice, that He said "never again will I curse the ground because of man." A covenant thus came into being between God and man when Noah made this sacrifice.

When we are standing at the altar on our wedding day, we should be making the same sacrifice, a sacrifice that says I am willing to give what I have and who I am unto the Lord for my spouse so that God will show me how to love my spouse through the times when I don't find him or her lovable. The bible teaches us this sacrifice in MATTHEW 16:24–25:

I Thee Wed

Then Jesus said to his disciples, "If any of you wants to be my follower, you must give up your own way, take up your cross, and follow me. If you try to hang on to your life, you will lose it. But if you give up your life for my sake, you will save it."

This resistance to losing my life for God showed itself in our marriage on numerous occasions. In January 2009, right after we had our son, I was at a place of anger and disappointment with my husband. We didn't communicate well, which led me to act independently of him in our marriage. I believed that if I didn't make life happen for us, then it was not going to happen. Most times I didn't bother to confer with him to hear his thoughts about an issue that affected both of us. I felt that he just didn't have that get up and go and a genuine concern for making our marriage thrive. I would blame him for my control problems. This led to our arguing in private and eventually in front of our kids.

One day a couple of months later, I got a call from Billy at work. He had called twice on my cell phone and once on my work phone. When I finally reached him, he told me that he was in an accident with our daughter Kennedy. My heart dropped. He immediately reassured me that they were okay, but I didn't know what to think.

When I arrived on the scene my mom and dad were there. I looked across the street near where my dad was standing, and I saw my husband's car turned over in a ditch rammed against a light pole. I got out of my car and ran to the scene. I hugged Billy, but as I wrapped my arms around him, all I could smell was alcohol on his breath, so I went to check on our daughter. She was okay. She only had a small bump on the left side of her head, for which I was so grateful. They both had walked away from this accident. Billy couldn't explain what had happened other than that he had fallen asleep at the wheel. There were no other cars involved in the accident.

After leaving the scene, I was skeptical at what had happened. I knew in the back of my mind that Billy had been drinking and lost control of the car. Yet, I was trying to stay positive. The next day we discussed the accident and, as usual, it led to a heated argument.

During this time, I really didn't feel like I knew how to be a wife to someone whom I felt was intentionally destroying our marriage with his alcohol addiction and laziness, so I wouldn't allow him to have much of a say-so in our relationship. I tore him down so much with my words, that I thought one day the light would suddenly go on and he would realize that all of our problems were his fault and that he needed to repent.

I recall years before the accident when I wanted to buy a house. I had a big corporate job and was making a lot of money, and between the two of us, I had the best credit. I quickly found an area where I could build the house I wanted and told Billy about it. Without considering his thoughts, I talked him into it. It would be in my name anyway, so why did I need to get his buy-in, I thought.

This had been my mindset for years! I was not going to be controlled by another man if I could help it. My first marriage had instilled this mindset in me. It was so bad that I didn't know how to let go of this controlling and demeaning spirit. I would ask God how to do it, but on the other hand, I didn't stop long enough to hear His answer.

From the time Billy and I had started dating until February 2012 my first priority was my career and trying to figure out how to make a lot of money. I appreciated my husband, but I had a different type of energy and focus that I thought he did not understand or appreciate.

During all of this time I didn't make the sacrifices that I should have made before I said "I do" again. Our marriage at that time was just another chapter in my life, just another title that I carried. Yes, I was a wife, but a terrible one I came to realize.

Had I embraced MATTHEW 16:24–25, our marriage would have been different. If only I had taken the time to know myself and to release the baggage from my past hurts, our marriage would have been different. Had I stopped to realize that I had a dog in this fight just as my husband had and taken responsibility for my part, I know our marriage would have been different. Had I trusted God in all things and allowed Him to direct my path and teach me how to be a wife then, I know our marriage would have been different.

I encourage you to take heed of the Word of God and to be sure that you make the necessary sacrifice to uphold your marriage covenant. It will not be easy, and you must fight against your fleshly desires. It takes work and the ability to recommit to it daily.

In those moments when you don't feel like being a

wife, be a wife. At those times when you feel like giving up and walking out the door, stick and stay. When you feel like you're carrying the burden and weight of the marriage alone, cast your cares onto the Lord. He will help and give you the peace you so desire. Your willingness to make these sacrifices for the greater good of your union will be more than worth it.

Questions for You to Reflect On

1. Do you believe that you are in covenant with God and your spouse?

2. Has your marriage become more of a contract than a covenant?

3. Has your view of your marriage commitment changed over the years? If so, how?

4. What sacrifice have you made to each other in your marriage? In your opinion, has it been worth it?

Seeking God's Guidance Before We Say "I Do."

The importance of hearing from God before you exchange your vows cannot be overstated. In many instances, we find ourselves in situations that we did not think were destined for us. We enter relationships thinking that because the person we are attracted to shows love by taking good care of us at the moment, then he or she must be the "one." We may experience butterflies at the sight of them, but we have not prayed, prepared, planned, or pursued God's guidance before we say "yes" to the question when it is popped.

When I married the first time, I had not prayed and was not prepared. Yes, my parents had been happily married for many years, and I had them as Christian role models. However, when the time came, and I met someone who could provide for me financially and rescue me from my hometown of Nashville, I said "yes" to him and "goodbye" to my friends and family. I thought it would be my quick and smooth getaway. The move and new chapter in my life would change its trajectory, would fill the empty places in my heart, would be all that I dreamed of, which was just to be happy and not experience the constant criticism and judgment of others. So I told myself.

I have been a "preacher's kid" all my life, and it seemed that people always had something negative to say about my choices and way of life. For example, some would tell me, "You think you're better than us," or "You need to put some meat on your bones because you're too skinny," or even "You're just a pretty girl, what do you know!" These statements played a part in how I began to react to what happened to me.

I've always considered myself to be a "people person," but I was tired of trying to please everyone. I was acting one way around church friends, another way around college friends, and still another way around family. It became too much. I began to wonder who I was and lost my authentic self in the translation. Eventually, I got to the point where I didn't care what others thought about me. I was going to do what I wanted to do, when I wanted to do it, and how I wanted to do it. I was no longer willing to confine myself to living up to their expectations.

On that hot summer day in June 2001, when I got married for the first time, the only thought on my mind was "Am I really doing this?" I was young, 26 to be exact, but felt I had control of my life, and no one was going to tell me any differently. I had bridal shower after bridal shower and a large wedding party. The night of the wedding rehearsal when we were leaving and heading out for the evening and I walked out of the church, there was a brand new 2001 Honda Accord Coupe with a big red bow on top waiting outside for me. "Wow!" I said. Is that my car? All of my bridesmaids were looking at the car and then at me as they joined in my surprise. I was super excited. My soon-to-be-husband had surprised me with a car. This impending wedding was shaping up to be all that I could ever have dreamt of, the type of wedding that you see in the movies or in magazines, and it was all happening to me. "This is how you get married," I said to myself.

There were many emotions and feelings coursing through me during that wedding weekend. I even thought to myself, "Now what have you got to say!" I was proving to all the haters that were looking on. I had picked the right one. I was showing them that I was making the best decision for me. I couldn't wait to leave for my honeymoon in beautiful Jamaica and then move away to South Carolina, my new home. I didn't worry about the looks and comments from people: I just brushed them off, chalking it all up to pure jealousy. Had I been paying closer attention, however, I would have seen the looks of care and concern in their eyes that said, "We love you and just want the best for you." Yes, I should have stopped to realize that I was so focused on having the perfect wedding, that I didn't consider that this was meant to be forever. I should have listened to those I knew who loved me. Most of all, I should have sought God first. As scripture tells us in MATTHEW 6:32–33:

> ...your heavenly Father already knows all
> your needs. Seek the Kingdom of God above
> all else, and live righteously, and he will give
> you everything you need.

Five

By August 2001, we were newlyweds and had moved to Columbia, SC, which was more than eight hours away from my family and friends. It was all new for me: a new husband, new apartment, new car, and even a new dog: "Bailey!" It wasn't perfect by any means, but I had chosen that life and now it was time for me to live with my choice. I wanted to know for myself that I had the courage and intellect to make wise choices on my own and that they would work out for good.

Soon after the honeymoon and excitement of the wedding wore off, reality began to settle in. The marriage became verbally unhealthy, and I was unhappy, frustrated, and pressured to be someone I was not, and I soon realized that I had moved too fast in making that decision. The enemy had a foothold in my marriage that led me to isolation and infidelity, which is not God's will for marriage. I had come to the realization that I had to get out and go back home to Nashville for some reconciliation. I had to go back and face my family and friends to apologize for my hasty decision and for the way I had treated them. I had to admit to them that I was not myself.

I made a mistake because I did not seek God first. I didn't wait for Him to show me whom He had set aside for me to marry. I thought that God was moving a bit too slowly for my schedule. I wanted to snatch up this opportunity for a different type of life while the iron was hot. Meanwhile, the iron's being hot was a warning to me that I might get burned. I was not ready for marriage. Red flags were waving in my face and I still ignored them.

When the circumstances of life are not aligning in your

favor, pay close attention. It could very well be a sign of personal issues within yourself that must be resolved. God might be saying, "Not in your time, but my time; Not your will, but my will be done."

Keep in mind that this is not necessarily a "no," and that a "no" doesn't always mean never, it just means not yet. Don't ignore your instincts. God gave women this gift of instinct, which is equivalent to the gift of the Holy Spirit, and it will not lead you in the wrong direction.

As you grow spiritually and seek God's guidance, the Holy Spirit will begin to give you answers to questions that you have not even asked. It will send you confirmation deep in your heart, evidence that you didn't seek with your natural mind. Your heart will not steer you in the wrong direction. The Word of God teaches us that God's answers are "yes" and "amen." According to 2 CORINTHIANS 1:20:

> *For all of God's promises have been fulfilled in Christ with a resounding "Yes!" And through Christ, our "Amen" (which means "Yes") ascends to God for his glory.*

Seeking God's Word

Don't manipulate God's Word by twisting it to fit something that He is not telling you. Your foundation must be the Word of God. If we start from the Word, all of our decisions and reactions will always come from a place of truth and love.

After much reflection and healing from my first marriage, I could see where I went wrong and where I should have stood on God's Word for my life before taking such a step. It will be difficult for you to stand on the Word if you don't know it, and if you don't know the Word, it will be impossible to live by it. After all, once you say those words "until death do you part," you must mean just that, and not "until I get tired and marriage gets hard!"

During that time in my life I didn't think to seek wisdom about the true meaning of the marriage vow. I was focused entirely on the wedding day and having a beautiful ceremony, reception, and honeymoon. I didn't think about what I would say to my husband-to-be.

My father walked me down the aisle and then turned to face the congregation to officiate the ceremony. It was then when he began to review the vows that I faced the question of whether I had made the right choice. But after seeing all the invited guests looking at the two of us, the doubt immediately took flight and I said to myself, "Oh well," and then aloud, "I do." I don't know that I even heard what my father was saying about the vows. Or that I understood the serious nature of the promise I was making before God and all those witnesses.

Now, when Billy and I got married, I remember a conversation with my maid of honor who stood up with me for both weddings. We were sitting in the hair salon the morning of the big day. I mentioned to her that Billy and I had decided to write our vows. She said, "Okay. Where are they?" My response was that I hadn't even started on them. She stared at me in disbelief. She reached down into my purse and tore out a sheet of paper from a pad and I began to share the words in my heart while she jotted them down.

I Thee Wed

I knew that, while I wouldn't remember everything she had written down, I'd have some idea of what I wanted to say to Billy, which were these words:

> We are here today in the presence of our Lord, and I want to take this time to let you know how much I love you and thank you for all that you have given me. I remember when we first met and how you showed me how to love again. I want to thank you for that. It was tough for me. I am so glad that you showed me how to open up. For that I thank you. You are a great man, and I can't wait to spend the rest of my life with you. You have been a good friend, supporter, and father to my daughter, and because of you, we have been able to unite our daughters to make one happy family. I thank you for that. Few men can do what you have done. I promise from this day forth to be faithful, to love you, to be patient through the good times and the bad. I love you with every breath that I take, and I mean it from the bottom of my heart. This is my solemn vow to you.

When I look back on that day, I can't help but to think that it was only God who put us together and brought us through. We still had some growing to do as a couple, and I was not pleased with everything that happened during our dating season, but God showed me the potential of who Billy could become and how he would teach me how to love again. I meant every word I spoke on that day.

Five

God's Love Is Sufficient

I come from a family that I knew loved me. They would express that love through their gifts and by providing for me. We were not always the touchy feely kind of family, but I had no doubt that my family loved me. I never had the feeling of being unloved by others growing up in the Baptist Church where I was a member of the "first family." This title came with benefits. As the church's first family, members often expressed how much they loved us. They would shower us with gifts and dinners. This tradition lasted until I became an adult.

All this attention and first-class service was the beginning of a behavior that I am not proud of. This, along with my parents giving me what I asked for, created a spirit of selfishness in me. I persuaded people to believe that it would either be my way or the highway.

Growing up I didn't realize that God loved me first and because of that love, I am able to love in return. Scripture teaches us in 1 CORINTHIANS 13:4 that love does not boast and it is not proud, nor is it self-seeking. This ignorance of knowing how to extend love led me into a marriage that was not right for me, and it cost me friends. It's been one of the most expensive lessons I have ever had to learn. This scripture describes God's love so clearly:

> May you experience the love of Christ, though
> it is too great to understand fully. Then you
> will be made complete with all the fullness of
> life and power that comes from God.
> — *EPHESIANS 3:19*

When you receive this revelation, you will be able to treat others the way you want to be treated. You will willingly extend love and grace unto others without looking for something in return.

With the love of God, you will know where your source of love comes from, and you will not look to others to fill that void. To quote writer C.S. Lewis, "When I have learnt to love God better than my earthly dearest, I shall love my earthly dearest better than I do now."

Questions for You to Reflect On

1. Did you wait to hear from God before you decided to marry?

2. Are you confident that God has said "Yes" to your union? What makes you confident?

3. Are you convinced that you made the right choice in a marriage partner? Why?

4. In what ways have you personally experienced God's love for you?

Six

Overcoming Strongholds
in Our Marriage

Before my marriage to Yolanda, God was nowhere in my decision to marry. I was motivated by selfish desires and had no concept of being head of the household as scripture teaches us in 1 CORINTHIANS 11:3:

> *But there is one thing I want you to know: The head of every man is Christ, the head of woman is man, and the head of Christ is God.*

Without God, the devil has an open-door policy to sow seeds of destruction in your marriage. Christ's protection in leading me was lacking because I did not look to Him. I was walking in darkness and my addiction to alcohol allowed the devil to hold me tighter in his grip. This dependency was the cause of many of the decisions I made during my first marriage. It led to arguments, anger, selfishness, neglect, and infidelity. The spirit of God was neither the foundation of, nor a part of, my decision to get married. Ultimately, because of this, the devil had control of the marriage and its eventual dissolution.

During that time in my life, after seeking God's

guidance, I was blessed to find a great church where I would meet my future wife and marry her four years later. When I married Yolanda, we were counseled by her father, our pastor. There was no question that God would be the foundation of our marriage.

So what went wrong in the beginning? The problem was that I had maintained old tendencies that I had brought to the doorstep of Yolanda's heart. My natural self was fighting the new spiritual man that I was becoming and my natural self was winning. That grip Satan had on me was too strong for me to fight by myself though I had convinced myself and tried to convince others that I had control of my habits. At the time, I refused to let anyone help me, even God.

In addition, I had a problem with anger management, where I would lose control when Yolanda and I would argue. She would come home from work and confront me about the smell of alcohol on my breath and how my skin reeked with it. It made me angry. She would find empty bottles that I thought I had hidden well and would confront me about them. I would explode in anger in an attempt to defend my drinking.

One night, I became so angry that I punched a hole in the wall outside our bedroom. After every argument, I would apologize and tell her that I would not drink again. But in my mind I knew it was a lie.

Another night, I threw a plate in the sink and broke it. My anger never got physical to the point where I would put my hands on Yolanda, but at times she would tell me that I made her afraid.

As men we often don't realize that there comes a point in our angry outbursts when we become frightening to those who love us, to those who look to us for security. When our wives observe the very men they look to for security turn on them with a viciousness that they would normally direct to a threat to their family, it can change the way our spouse views us from then on. It's a reaction you don't want to see in your marriage.

My anger and my dependence on alcohol were shortcomings in my life that the natural man within me allowed to grow out of control. Addiction is nothing more than loyalty to an idol, an idol that refuses to be second to anything. The devil realizes this and understands the power God has in joining a man and a woman whom He has ordained to be married. Destroying this union is the devil's mission, and he will use any and every tool he can to accomplish it. With our marriage, the devil saw an easy way to do this.

Although I recognized the spirit in our relationship when Yolanda and I exchanged vows on our wedding day, I did not respect them enough to remain obedient to them after our wedding day. This disobedience kept me from realizing that I could not break free from this grip alone. I needed God's help. I had to acknowledge that God is in control, and evidence of that control is the woman He placed in my life.

When we come before God and witnesses on our wedding day, we must be mindful of what we are asking of God in blessing our marriage, and we must be fully conscious of what we are promising. We have come before

God out of respect for who He is and in obedience to what He commanded of us. When we stand before God as a couple, we symbolize to the world our public declaration that we are standing on God's promise that the "two shall become one."

This is not something to be taken lightly, and we should come before God with eagerness and in peace. We should come knowing that after this vow is exchanged, God will bless our union and do great work through us for His glory. No other cares or worries should occupy our minds or hearts. This is the time when:

> *... A man leaves his father and mother and is joined to his wife, and the two are united into one.*
> —*EPHESIANS 5:31*

When you tell your wife that you love her, you are also telling God that you love His blessing. Conversely, when a wife tells her husband that she is looking forward to a life with him, she is telling God that she accepts the journey with this man whom God has sent with His blessings and guidance.

Whatever you pledge to each other in your vow, you are pledging it to God as well. You make the vow knowing that your union is a foundation for the service of our Lord. We must make sure that the spiritual is respected in this union because if the vows are made to each other only because they sound good, feel good, or make you look good, or any other worldly reason, God is excluded from the ceremony, and the relationship will be at the mercy of the world and its ruler.

You came into this world through the seed God placed inside of your parents. You were nurtured and cared for and protected by one or both of them. As you began to grow, you were taught how to live, survive, and were educated with the knowledge of how to face the world. Once you became an adult, you put off those childish ways and took on the responsibilities of an adult. This commitment to your marriage is an adult reaction to love as you see it and believe in it.

Now, before God, you solemnly swear to protect and cover another person as you both plant a seed in the ground together. This seed will be nurtured and cultivated. It will be cherished and honored. It will have the potential to produce offspring. It will withstand the winds and the rain, the storms, and other natural disasters because it is a seed of faith, trust, and hope. This is what you are promising to God to accomplish through your marriage.

A married couple may not remember or understand the vow they made before God and how serious the promise is. For this reason, we should always seek His wisdom before making such a commitment. It's not about a diamond ring and a sheet of parchment that says you are now legally man and wife and can live in the same house. You are speaking from the spirit and proclaiming to God that you promise to love Him first and keep His commands for your marriage.

Although Yolanda and I prepared our vows at the last minute, we meant every word that we said to each other. We are thankful that we had the opportunity to record them. Up to this day, we go back and listen to them every now and then. That's why it is our life's mission and purpose to encourage other married and engaged couples to remember what they promised and to renew their commitment to each other. After all, Jesus didn't make us a promise and then at the point of crucifixion, back out. No, He came to the earth for a mission. He loves us so much that He laid down His life for our sins. He told the Disciples that He had come to fulfill the promise of God:

God is not a man, so he does not lie.
He is not human, so he does not change his mind.
Has he ever spoken and failed to act?
Has he ever promised and not carried it through?
— NUMBERS 23:19

And who are Jesus's friends? We, the children of God, are His friends. God is calling married people to demonstrate that same commitment and desire to lay down their lives for a friend, who, in this sense, is your spouse. Will you lay down your life for him or her?

When you are making a vow to God to "have and to hold, to love and to cherish, in sickness and in health, for richer or poorer, for better or for worse, so long as you both shall live," you are declaring that divorce is not an option! A failed marriage is not an option! In making this vow, standing on God's promise and trusting in His word, know that nothing will come between your union. Remain always obedient, and what has been ordained, will remain so. Seek God's wisdom first. Know that He has plans to prosper you, and He will bring that right person along for courtship and then marriage in His time.

Questions for You to Reflect On

1. What characteristics of you that are not of God are you aware must be shed for your marriage to prosper?

2. What aspects of your natural life have to be overcome in order for your spiritual self to be aligned with God?

3. How has God worked through you as a couple to further His Kingdom?

4. Do you feel that you understand your vows better today than when you first recited them? Why or why not?

Miracles and Second Chances in Our Marriage

I began to observe a peaceful change in Yolanda. She was studying and praying every day. There were no longer arguments with me about my drinking. It was almost like it didn't bother her anymore. It made me think. What is going on? Shortly thereafter, I realized that she had let it go and gave it up to God. I could see it in her worship and her excitement for preaching the Gospel.

By January 2013, we both started leading the "Feed Your Faith" new members' class at our church. Then, by that summer, we took our first long road trip together to Dallas and attended the T.D. Jakes Pastors and Leaders Conference. During the twelve hours it took to drive there and back, we were able to reflect on our marriage and our future.

Soon after, Yolanda and I started attending bible study at our church. I began to read the bible study guide that was designed for the classes. What I liked about it was that it had scriptures for each day of the week. I grew into the habit of reading the scripture of the day. Eventually, I would read the entire chapter that contained that scripture of the day. This began to increase my devotional time with the Lord.

I was developing a habit of studying the Word on a daily basis. This habit would eventually allow for the Holy Spirit in me to pray for what I could not pray for on my own. One day that cloud of a "lie" disappeared—the lie that I had been telling myself and others. Staying in the scriptures helped me to better understand God's Word and how it pertained to my life. This evolving knowledge began to bring all things in darkness to light.

Although I was in the Word, my addiction to alcohol had still not ceased entirely. After work one day, I cracked the seal on a bottle of my drink of choice. As I began to twist off the cap, I stopped, looked at the bottle and thought, "I'm going to drink this for the rest of my life." It was at that moment when I realized that I had a problem and didn't know how to stop. A few days later, on Wednesday, September 11, 2013 when I opened my Bible to read the scripture of the day, DEUTERONOMY 30:15:

> *"Now listen! Today I am giving you a choice between life and death, between prosperity and disaster...."*

A feeling of discomfort came over me. I didn't know it then, but I was uncomfortable because the spirit in me was fighting the natural me. I continued reading, and that scripture stayed with me.

Ten days later, I was riding my motorcycle down a two-lane interstate when a small pickup truck lost control and spun out in the distance ahead. I thought the truck would come to a rest before we were to pass it. I was riding in front and Yolanda was on her motorcycle behind me with a friend tailing her. They quickly swerved to the right in order to get out of the way, but I didn't, and the truck hit me.

I don't remember what happened after that because I blacked out. Waking up in the hospital and seeing the faces of family, friends, and doctors, I lost consciousness again, yet I remember the scripture that was in my head and on my heart. I cried out with conviction, "I choose life! My God in heaven, I choose life!"

The Light That Shines Through Us

After my motorcycle accident, I experienced three miracles:

- I didn't die. God spared my life and gave me another chance at this life.

- God allowed me to remain in my right mind and God healed my body.

- He took away the craving I had for alcohol.

Yolanda describes the collision that I had as terrifying. She saw me get hit and what was left of the broken bone sticking out of my pants as I lay in the street. I would hear story after story of how I looked immediately after the accident. Co-workers who came to see me said they did not see any sign that I would recover from my injuries. The doctors themselves had sought the right words to console me to make me feel better about my situation. The very first thing I was told by the doctors was that I would lose my leg.

But God's healing hand was at work as the doctor made

that prognosis. As the team of doctors reconstructed my leg, replacing the crushed bone with metal and screws, the concern was whether the replaced tissue would be accepted by my body. I was in severe pain and heavily medicated so I recalled very little of the reconstruction process. I left my healing in God's hands.

The healing was evident the day I saw my leg without the bandage for the first time after the accident. Up until then, whenever they took my leg brace and bandages off, I had to be anesthetized. But on that particular day, the doctors said that I had healed enough so that it wasn't necessary to put me under. When the nurse unwrapped the bandages, what I saw frightened me. As a homicide detective for the city of Nashville, I had witnessed some gruesome scenes that never made me feel queasy or caused me to turn away. But when a part of my own body was laid open for me to see, it was a whole different matter.

My right leg looked like it had been mauled by a bear. I saw the flesh and blood dripping on the table I was lying on. No way did it look like I was healing! I looked up at the doctors who were, at the time, shaking hands and congratulating each other. "Are you serious?" I asked, looking at the leg. One of the younger doctors came to me, and with a smile, informed me that the bleeding was a good thing because it meant that my replaced tissue had been accepted by my body. My healing was going as planned.

I realized that I couldn't see it because my mind was mired in doubt. It was only when I accepted the fact that God was in control and surrendered to Him that He took over and brought me through. While the doctors were congratulating themselves, it occurred to me that if they were God-fearing men, they knew that God guided their hands during my eight surgeries.

As I continued to heal, the doctors were surprised at my rapid progress and what I was able to do. My insurance provided only for short term disability, which meant that I couldn't be off work more than six months. The doctors told me that I would require several years of healing before I could be anything close to normal again, but I was back at work, full time, although on light duty and on crutches a few weeks short of six months. I had only God to thank for that miracle!

My co-workers who saw me in the hospital just after the accident couldn't believe what they saw, knowing what I looked like before the accident and afterwards. They were amazed at my transformation, but I knew what they really saw in me was my transformation due to God's healing hands. His grace and mercy gave me the strength I needed to endure. What I prayed that everyone saw in me was God's presence in my life, a light for others to see as they witnessed my journey to recovery—the hope that is within me, a hope that I share with others, then unconsciously, but now as a living, open testament.

It was then that I promised God that I would follow His commands, train myself to follow all of them, and obey Him, as expressed in 1 CORINTHIANS 9:27:

> *I discipline my body like an athlete, training it to do what it should. Otherwise, I fear that after preaching to others I myself might be disqualified.*

Seven

When I surrendered that day in the hospital, God took my addiction away. The impossible was made possible. In spite of the life I was living, the liquor I was worshiping, and my neglect of the wife God had blessed me with, He gave me another chance. He laid His loving and healing hands on me and my family and turned around a situation that seemed impossible.

It is a blessing from God for a man and woman to be married. Marriage was created and instituted by God signifying the relationship between Christ and the Church. If God has called you to be married, you must honor the call, knowing that He has blessed your union and the togetherness you vow to keep. For when God created man, He decreed that man should not be alone (GENESIS 2:18), so He created woman out of the man's rib (GENESIS 2:21–22):

> *So the LORD God caused the man to fall into a deep sleep. While the man slept, the LORD God took out one of the man's ribs and closed up the opening. Then the Lord God made a woman from the rib, and he brought her to the man.*

God ordained marriage, and Adam and Eve were created first as a blessing to the earth. This was not the only time God's ordination for marriage is revealed. It is shown again when God sent His one and only Son to the earth to begin His ministry. Confirming the significance that God has accorded married life, the very first miracle Jesus performed was during a wedding, at Cana. Jesus's mother and his disciples were invited to the wedding as well.

I Thee Wed

Scripture tells us:

> *The next day there was a wedding celebration in the village of Cana in Galilee. Jesus' mother was there, and Jesus and his disciples were also invited to the celebration. The wine supply ran out during the festivities, so Jesus' mother told him, "They have no more wine."*
>
> *"Dear woman, that's not our problem," Jesus replied. "My time has not yet come." But his mother told the servants, "Do whatever he tells you."*
>
> *Standing nearby were six stone water jars, used for Jewish ceremonial washing. Each could hold twenty to thirty gallons. Jesus told the servants, "Fill the jars with water." When the jars had been filled, he said, "Now dip some out, and take it to the master of ceremonies." So the servants followed his instructions.*
>
> *When the master of ceremonies tasted the water that was now wine, not knowing where it had come from (though, of course, the servants knew), he called the bridegroom over.*
> *— JOHN 2:1–9*

Seven

This is a miracle: water turned to wine at a wedding. Jesus knew the importance of marriage, so he worked a miracle among the people to signify it. Jesus tells his mother that it is not yet his time, but still the miracle takes place. This makes it even more obvious that God favors and desires marriage. And it's why the following words are said during the ceremony:

> *"…let no one split apart what God has joined together."*
> — MARK 10:9

For the newly married couple, it means not giving up. Not giving in to the world, but keeping God as your foundation in everything you do together in marriage. The joy that the two of you share should be already rooted. The excitement of the journey should be your focus, not the excitement of the day, for it's after the wedding day that the journey serving God as a couple begins. The fruits of your union are dependent on how the two of you make the transition of becoming one. But do not worry. Remember to keep God as the foundation of your marriage, and with obedience, the transition will happen.

Questions for You to Reflect On

1. Do you believe that God has ordained your marriage? Why do you believe that?

2. What miracle have you experienced during the course of your relationship?

3. Have you surrendered your will to God? When did you do so, and what were the circumstances surrounding it?

4. In what way is God the foundation of your marriage?

Surrendering to
God in Our Marriage

On the outside, my marriage with Billy appeared one way to others, but on the inside it was another story. I occupied myself in my career and my own personal life and just soldiered on in spite of the problems that beset us as a couple. I just kept thinking that this, too, shall pass. In the beginning I thought I could change Billy singlehandedly and cure him of his addiction to alcohol. I had failed to realize that the history of alcoholism in my own family ended in tragedy.

The belief that I could change his behavior stayed with me until I just finally gave up. At that point, all I could do was keep my head up in front of our kids and everyone around us. This went on for years. Frustrated that I couldn't change him, I tried everything I could to fix myself and find my own purpose. I went on meditation retreats, self-help conferences, took classes, saw a psychologist, and even sought out the counsel of New Age spiritual advisors and self-improvement coaches.

Eventually, I came to the point where none of these options worked and I couldn't take it anymore, and I threatened to leave. I grew tired of finding bottles he had hidden all over the house, in the garage, and under the beds. I was leaving him because it was all his fault. He was ruining my life and our kids' lives because of his habit. I couldn't confide in anyone because he was a police officer and this issue would jeopardize his job. To make matters worse, he was a deacon in my father's church, and we had an image to uphold.

One day, while at work, I told Billy that I needed to go away for a couple of days. With no clear destination in mind, I needed to get away from it all. I ended up traveling to a bed and breakfast on the top of Lookout Mountain in Chattanooga, Tennessee.

It was there that I had a "come to Jesus" moment, where I poured out my heart to God and emptied my frustrations, insecurities, hurts, fears, and guilt at His feet. Things surfaced from my childhood that I had been carrying into my adult life. It was there where I released the hurt and failures in my life and stopped asking "why" and "how" and started saying "yes, I surrender."

Immediately after I returned home from the time away, on a bright and sunny February Sunday morning of 2012, I had my first real spiritual encounter with God, and it was then that I stopped running, stopped trying to control my destiny and the destinies of others—including my husband's. I gave it all up and totally surrendered. This spiritual enlightenment led me to finally accepting the call from God, which was to preach and to teach the Gospel of Jesus Christ. I clearly heard the Lord say, "help the people," and from that point on, that was my only mission. Not even two weeks after, God spoke very clearly to my spirit and said: "What you resist will grow stronger if you fail to deal with it."

God was ready for me to go. But, I quickly realized that I didn't know enough about the bible to teach others, so in the fall of 2012, I enrolled in school at Union University where after two years I earned a Master's in Christian Studies. This was another example of how God literally walked me through step by step in order to accomplish His will for my life. One of the areas I had to shed in that season of surrender was realizing that I am smart and God has instilled in me all that it takes to fulfill His mission for my life. I just needed to trust Him.

All of those years during my marriage, I had been pointing at my husband because of his addiction and what it was doing to me and our family, when in reality I, too, was an addict. My addiction was not a chemical dependency, but it was an addiction nonetheless—to selfishness, control, and insecurity in who I was in Christ. My addiction put our family in debt and kept us in that place of not having enough. I had spent thousands and thousands of dollars chasing worldly wealth and success. Nothing would stop me from spending this money and putting the kids off on my parents just to get what "I" wanted. I was looking at life through 3D glasses. Everyone looked so much bigger than me, and all I saw was my lack, my not enough and my fears. Instead of seeing myself as fearfully and wonderfully made with a purpose and destiny that God has predestined for my life. I was trying to be big in the world and not big for God. Until I faced this fact and admitted it to myself, I realized nothing was ever going to change for the better until I looked in the mirror to change me. I was the problem! That is when the "sanctification" process began in my life.

I immersed myself in the Word. I prayed consistently for my husband and our marriage, asking God to fix my heart, create in me a clean heart and renew the right spirit in me. I started speaking the Word over my life, marriage, and kids and stopped directly blaming them for my problems. When I would come home and catch Billy in the act of drinking, I would not get angry or mad as I had done in the past. I would peacefully walk away and allow God to deal with him. God had filled my heart with peace, and the joy of the Lord became my strength.

I was being transformed, and soon after, delivered from my problems. I became kinder and more compassionate to those I loved. I relinquished all control unto God—so much so that I began to wake up each day and ask Him, "How can I be of service today?" I discarded my plans and dreams and accepted God's plan and provision for my life. The pressure of trying to prove my value to others was melting away. I learned who I am in Christ and have held onto it since then. The scripture found in PROVERBS 4:7 says it best.

> *Getting wisdom is the wisest thing you can do! And whatever else you do, develop good judgment.*

I was finally gaining the wisdom, knowledge, and understanding that was needed to be married and, most of all, to stay married.

Eight

More than a year after Billy's motorcycle accident, the Lord taught me another great lesson that I treasure as the biggest lesson of my life. It was now up to me to care for my husband as he began the healing process. He was as helpless as a baby. We created a makeshift hospital room in our living room because he could not climb the stairs to our bedroom. I had to cook, clean, bathe him and change his wound dressings as well as take care of our kids for months.

I learned how to maneuver my husband around the house so that he would be comfortable and have access to what he needed. I recall rolling him in the wheelchair to the bathroom where I had to help him use it—a humbling experience for both of us. Night after night, I would fall on my bed exhausted, forced to sleep alone while thinking to myself, "This too shall pass." Bear in mind that I had worked in my corporate job all day. It felt as though I had two full-time jobs, working 17-to-18-hour shifts. When I think about it now, without this challenge to my faith and the humility forced upon me, I might still be struggling with self-centered ambitions and a lack of wholeness in my marriage.

I was reminded of the time when Jesus washed the feet of his disciples in John, Chapter 13, where scripture teaches us that when Jesus was preparing to depart from them to be with God, they were having their last meal in the Upper Room. After the feast, Jesus rose and began to pour water into a basin, and while using the towel around His waist, he began washing their feet one at a time. This was considered to be a lowly task that only servants would perform and is one of the most explicit lessons of servanthood and humility that we can learn from our Lord and Savior Jesus Christ.

In marriage, we must have a spirit of humility to serve our spouse, just as Jesus did. As wives, we have been created to be the helpmeet to our husbands, as according to GENESIS 2:18:

> Then the LORD God said, "It is not good for
> the man to be alone. I will make a helper
> who is just right for him."

Being a humble servant must be our focus and our goal in our marriage. As spouses we must never ignore the opportunities to serve our mates with a spirit of humility. Doing so will provide an extra measure of purpose and fulfillment in your marriage.

Questions for You to Reflect On

1. What areas in your life are hindering you from living out God's plan and purpose for you?

2. What do you think is God's mission for your life?

3. What are you resisting that God is asking you to face?

4. What has been the biggest lesson God has taught you along your marriage journey?

The Role of Witnesses in Our Marriage

There are times in a relationship when we notice characteristics in our significant others that we either didn't see at first, or noticed but turned a blind eye to them at the time. What we men must realize is that when we are single, we learn ways of the world that benefit us according to our own needs and motives. We are living for our own individual selves. As saved individuals, however, we must allow God to transform our natural selves into our spiritual selves. Scripture teaches us in ROMANS 12:2:

> *Don't copy the behavior and customs of this world, but let God transform you into a new person by changing the way you think. Then you will learn to know God's will for you, which is good and pleasing and perfect.*

Of the many things that could fall under "God's perfect will," marriage is one of them. Some of the characteristics we have acquired over the course of our lives must be shed. They should no longer be a part of us because they are not of God; nor are they for His purpose and glory. So, when our wives address something unbecoming in us, we shouldn't automatically respond with the words, "You knew I was like this when you met me!" "This is who I am!"

Think about God's purpose and His communication to you, through your wife, to get rid of that personality trait. There is a "new you" that He wants to use. For Him to be able to do that, you must discard all in you that is not of God.

Being Accountable to Your Witnesses

There will be seasons when your vows will be tested, seasons when you will need to lean on each other and seek God's wisdom for guidance. You may need to be reminded by the witnesses who stood up with you at your wedding to encourage you along the way. You both were declaring to them that you need their prayers and help to strengthen your marriage in times of weakness. This is why you chose them to be a part of the wedding party. It's why they were asked to wear special attire that they may never wear again. The positions in which they stand as a part of the wedding party can and will be uncomfortable at times. After all, you don't need "yes" men or women. You need witnesses to cover you and hold you accountable to the promise you made to each other and to God.

When the two of you don't see eye to eye, you must be able to turn to those witnesses, who should be willing to stand up for what is right and remind you that you both must submit to the Lord. A wife may need to be reminded that the husband is the head of the household, and therefore is her provider and protector—even though he may not be displaying the characteristics of Jesus at that moment. You both must be reminded that love is a verb. This scripture from ECCLESIASTES 4:9–10 explains it all:

> *Two people are better off than one, for they can help each other succeed. If one person falls, the other can reach out and help. But someone who falls alone is in real trouble.*

A husband and wife don't need witnesses who do not adhere to the Word. They must be righteous, spiritually grounded, and willing to call us out when we have stepped out of bounds. There should be someone in your life who can step in and hold you accountable. Someone from whom you can seek wise counsel. That person should be there to speak life to your spirit. But God, through the power of the Holy Spirit, is the only One who can transform your heart, and He will bring things back into remembrance for you.

This is what your wedding vows must be for the witnesses at your wedding. They must be the beginning of that light that will shine as a result of your union. As you live out your marriage, everyone who witnessed your beginning should rejoice in its fruits.

It does not matter whether you as a couple are encountered daily by your witnesses or not. What God has ordained by your union will come to fruition. Therefore, it is critical to keep God as the foundation of your marriage, for your marriage is the hope that others will see and praise God for as they embark on their own marriages. This is how the love and the glory of God can become contagious and spread. MATTHEW 5:14–16 says:

> *You are the light of the world—like a city on a hilltop that cannot be hidden. No one lights a lamp and then puts it under a basket. Instead, a lamp is placed on a stand, where it gives light to everyone in the house. In the same way, let your good deeds shine out for all to see, so that everyone will praise your heavenly Father.*

The city situated on a hill metaphor symbolizes that pledging of your lives to each other through your wedding vows is the center of the ceremony. What the two of you feel for each other should manifest itself in both of you. God's blessing of the love you have for each other should shine brightly giving "…light for all who are in the house." After the ceremony, your guests should take away this light of hope in the joy they see in the two of you.

Questions for You to Reflect On

1. What characteristics about yourself that are not of God of which you are aware must be shed?

2. How willing are you to accept counsel from the witnesses who stood up for you at your wedding?

3. How does your marriage manifest itself to others as a light that shines through you?

Ten

Achieving a Purpose-Filled Marriage

As Billy and I began to focus on strengthening our life together, we discovered the purpose for our marriage. God created man and woman and commanded them to carry out two specific functions: procreation, which is to be fruitful and to multiply and to rule over the earth and thereby subdue it. It is made clear in GENESIS 1:28:

> *Then God blessed them and said, "Be fruitful*
> *and multiply. Fill the earth and govern it.*
> *Reign over the fish in the sea, the birds in the*
> *sky, and all the animals that scurry along the*
> *ground."*

As a married couple, we are duty bound to produce fruit. What fruit, you may ask? Fruit that represents the Fruits of the Spirit found in GALATIANS 5:22–23.

> *But the Holy Spirit produces this kind of fruit*
> *in our lives: love, joy, peace, patience,*
> *kindness, goodness, faithfulness, gentleness,*
> *and self-control. There is no law against these*
> *things!*

A tree is known by the fruit it bears. Likewise, your marriage will be known by the fruit that you bear together. This brings us back to the scripture from GENESIS 1:28, which proclaims that marriage is also created to multiply the earth. Multiplication starts with a husband and a wife who join to become one sexually with the intention of procreating. For our offspring, it is our responsibility to be living examples of Christ on earth. Therefore, we must teach them to love God and obey His commands. By doing this, we fill the earth with the good fruit that the Spirit commands of us as followers of Christ.

Marriage has a great purpose with very specific instructions. Often, we miss the purpose and allow the systems of the world to determine what and how our marriage should be. It is God's plan and desire for us to return to Eden and live a life of wholeness and obedience to each other just as it was intended for Adam and Eve before the Fall of Man. Every day that we wake up, this should be our focus and mission for our marriage, so that ultimately our marriage becomes a process of spiritual refinement in which we as husband and wife united in holy matrimony reflect God's greatness. We will never get to this place if we are not equally yoked and are not of one accord on this mission.

To fuel your marriage and keep it thriving, you must have a burning passion to love your spouse and look forward to seeing what God has done and is doing through them. In this regard, it is important that you study your spouse. What does it mean to study him or her? You must understand your mate's strengths, weaknesses, areas of

Ten

opportunity for growth and their trigger points.

As wives we must exercise our strengths in order to complement our husbands. We must come to the marriage as a "whole" person so we are able to love out of our overflow. We can't pour into our spouse from a half-empty cup.

Another way to study your spouse is to discover his or her love language. *The Five Love Languages*, by Dr. Gary Chapman, includes a brief assessment that you can take that will give you insights on how your spouse best receives love. Knowing this can be a game changer for a marriage.

Reading the book and taking the assessment confirmed what I always knew about my husband Billy. His love language is quality time because he loves to spend time together. By that I mean time when we have each other's undivided attention. I love spending time with him as well because he is my best friend and lover.

Sometimes though, I like to multi-task and might be on my phone or might send an email or two in the middle of our date or movie night. As you might guess, that doesn't go over well when spending quality time together is your mate's love language. I had to learn to put away all distractions and just focus on him. These moments should be cherished in a marriage. We should be grateful and excited that we get to date our spouse as a married couple just as we placed such a high priority on dating during our courtship.

Marriage was created and ordained by God to be a blessing for His people. When God said that man shall not be alone, it was meant to:

- Protect us from feelings of loneliness.

- Protect women from danger and violence.

- Provide for sexual intimacy between a husband and wife.

- Enhance our resources as part of God's plan for us.

All of these are blessings and benefits of Christian marriage as expressed in PSALM 103:2:

> Let all that I am praise the LORD; may I never forget the good things he does for me.

If only we could shift our mindset to understand and focus on the blessing that the institution of marriage is, we would be able to keep our vow to our spouse and God. We should spend time reflecting on the blessings that God has bestowed on our marriage, taking the time to assess its mission. Are you moving closer to Christ or farther away?

Your marriage should be the driving force that brings you and your spouse to the feet of Jesus. In doing so, you must be prepared to resist the "drift effect," the consequence of not investing the time and resources necessary for your marriage to prosper. This happens when you are not fully present in your marriage and fulfilling your obligation as husband and wife.

When you and your husband exchanged your vows, you also made a commitment to God. With that in mind, you must accept the fact that your union comes with an obligation, an obligation that is bigger than the two of you.

Ten

How the both of you live, how the both of you appear to the outside world, and how you cope during your trials together are all part of your obligation. In JOHN 13:34, Jesus says,

> *So now I am giving you a new*
> *commandment: Love each other. Just as I*
> *have loved you, you should love each other.*

This is not a request from Jesus; nor is it a suggestion. It is a command that we love one another. It is our individual obligation. Jesus wants us to love just as He loved us. Now, take the same love that Jesus showed us as He was beaten, bruised and scorned. This was a selfless act of love. Imagine that kind of love and sacrifice being given to each other every day of your marriage! It's called sacrificial love, which is our obligation as a married couple. Your marriage is bigger than just the two of you, and you have an obligation to live out Christ's command in your marriage. By doing so, you will remain faithful to your obligations to each other as husband and wife. These obligations fall into three areas: spiritual, emotional, and physical. Let's unpack them by first reflecting on this scripture from EPHESIANS:

> *A man leaves his father and mother and is*
> *joined to his wife, and the two are united into*
> *one. This is a great mystery, but it is an*
> *illustration of the way Christ and the church*
> *are one.*
> *— EPHESIANS 5:31–32*

The Spiritual Obligation

The first obligation for marriage is to be spiritually connected. If you want to know how your spouse is feeling or what he or she is going through, listen actively and observe his or her behavior. There will be times when words are left unspoken, but you can sense something is amiss by your spouse's observable behavior. Try to assess the situation so that you can get to the root cause of the issue. In some instances, being fully present and showing that you care may be the only requirement that is needed.

One weekend when Billy and I were preparing to teach a class on marriage, we had planned to sit down and walk through our talking points. When we got to the office and began to review our work, I noticed that he was not in a good spiritual place. I saw the tension in his face and demeanor, so I asked him if he were okay. Of course, he said "yes," but I looked at him and I asked him "how is your heart tonight?" That failed to get him to open up as well. He said that he didn't want to talk about it.

Now, I can be persistent, but I knew that he didn't want to talk, so I pushed our work aside and sat there with him quietly for a moment. I told him that our marriage is our first priority. We could not continue working with other couples on their marriages when there's an imbalance in ours.

Later, he opened up to me about an issue that he was dealing with and we talked through it. Afterwards, with God's strength and guidance, we were able to successfully complete the task at hand. This is a perfect example of not putting off concerns in your relationship to accomplish something that lies outside of it. Had I not been spiritually connected to my husband, I would have missed the opportunity to help him resolve the problem.

Here are some tips to keep your marriage spiritually connected:

- Pray together daily for your marriage and others'.

- Spend time reading, studying, and sharing the Bible together.

- Attend church and seek an area to serve there together.

- Spend time with other godly couples and share best marriage practices.

- Keep dating each other!

Don't get discouraged if you can't participate in a daily prayer at first. These tips are provided here as goals to strive toward. Sit down together as often as you can at first, but commit yourselves to making progress until you reach your goal. You might start off at twice a week praying together. Later, move it up to three times a week, and so on. Soon, you will reach the goal of praying together every day. This also includes spending time reading and studying the Bible together. You goal is not only to have a spiritual experience with your spouse, it is also to increase the spirituality in general in your marriage.

It is important to your marriage to spend time with other godly couples. Often, we prefer to stay in our comfort zones, and, in this case, with our friends. Many of the couples that surround us are experiencing similar trials, and sometimes the challenges are the same. When you spend time with other couples who have survived rough patches in their marriages and have a victory in their testimony, not only can it give you direction and insight, but it can keep the hope ignited in your marriage. Along with the feeling that you and your spouse are not alone in your journey, you may begin to rediscover the purpose of your marriage. With this purpose, the journey will evolve from being a relationship that requires work, to one that you wake up to every day ready to build on and spread that light to others.

The Emotional Obligation

The second obligation in a marriage is for the two to be emotionally connected. We must always be available to guard each other's heart from hurt and show the love of Christ in the things we do and say.

Billy is always ready and positioned to guard my heart. There have been instances in my life where I have experienced hurt by someone outside of our marriage. For instance, I had experienced some negative feedback from my boss on my job that caught me off guard. I was sharing the conversation with Billy and told him how hurt I was from the feedback and how this particular feedback did not come across as constructive. In my mind, I began to think so negatively about what my boss said about me that I allowed it to attack my character.

Billy stopped me in my tracks and told me not to go there. He told me that I can't give someone that much power over me. If so, I was allowing him and not God to control me. Then he began to speak scripture into my heart, which blocked the enemy from trying to take over my mind and thoughts. I knew that I didn't deserve how I had been treated, and I know that I am more than a conqueror, but had it not been for my husband's spiritual wisdom and discernment, I would have let it get the best of me emotionally. To fulfill the emotional obligation in your marriage, you can do the following:

- Freely express verbal and physical affection toward one another.

- Have open and honest communication without fear of retaliation.

- Share concerns and seek solutions together.

- Accept constructive criticism without being defensive.

- Show vulnerability in times of weakness without being ashamed.

- Talk about everything!

As couples, we must keep a stable and healthy emotional connection in our marriage. If we don't, the chances for divorce will increase.

The Physical Obligation

The third obligation for a sound marriage is to be physically connected. We are not just talking about sex, although it is a very important part of the physical connection. Let's look at the non-sexual aspect first. Jimmy

Evans, an expert on Christian marriage and founder of The Marriage Today Ministry, says "When you are taking care of your marriage outside of the bedroom it will take care of itself inside of the bedroom."

This is the one area of marriage that sits on the shoulders of our past, depending on how we were raised, what we experienced during our childhood, and who taught us about love and sex. All of this follows you into your marriage.

Some spouses' love language is physical touch, while others' not so much. What we must understand is that physical touch is not just holding hands and draping your arm around your spouse's shoulder. That's needed too, but to strengthen our physical connection, we must be in tune with our spouse's entire body. You've no doubt heard the well-known saying, "The eyes are the window to the soul." This is true. If you relate to your spouse, you can gaze into his or her eyes and have a good sense of the state of your spouse's soul. This cannot happen if you don't spend time together and don't know your spouse's wants and needs. Here are five techniques that will keep you physically connected outside of the bedroom.

- Be fully present when you are together.
- Look your spouse in the eyes and smile routinely.
- Discover who your spouse is by asking what he or she likes and how he or she likes it.
- Learn your spouse's love language and speak it.
- Try showing physical affection that doesn't always lead to sex.

Ten

Being present to each other is very important. There is no substitute for being aware and available during quality time spent together. In other words, don't harbor ulterior motives, such as thinking, "I'm going to spend the day with my spouse, and that will free me up for some 'me' time later in the week." Know that you are with your spouse by listening to every word, watching all his or her moves and being conscious of how he or she is responding to being with you.

If you show attention that warrants affection, you will receive the same in return. This is the best time for being active in your spouse's love language, being proud and constantly grateful for and in the relationship you have with each other.

Now, sex, on the other hand, is a very important aspect of being connected physically and, yes, it is an obligation in marriage—one that you as husband and wife should enjoy! It is not to be used as a weapon against your spouse as a punishment; nor should it be used to fulfill lustful desires. Scripture teaches us in 1 CORINTHIANS 7:1–5:

Now regarding the questions you asked in your letter. Yes, it is good to abstain from sexual relations. But because there is so much sexual immorality, each man should have his own wife, and each woman should have her own husband.

The husband should fulfill his wife's sexual needs, and the wife should fulfill her husband's needs. The wife gives authority

*over her body to her husband, and the
husband gives authority over his body to his
wife.*

*Do not deprive each other of sexual relations,
unless you both agree to refrain from sexual
intimacy for a limited time so you can give
yourselves more completely to prayer.
Afterward, you should come together again
so that Satan won't be able to tempt you
because of your lack of self-control.*

Although this is not a book that delves deeply into the matter of sex, you cannot discuss your marriage obligation without addressing it. What Paul writes in this scripture is clear: our body is not our own. We should enjoy the creation of sexual intercourse as God designed it. Neglecting this aspect of your marriage will cause marital issues such as anger, resentment, low self-esteem, addiction to pornography, and of course, extramarital affairs. Don't fall into these traps of the enemy. Spend the time to be sexually present with your spouse. Moreover, don't compare your sex life to others. What works for you is for you.

Sex within marriage can be an open door leading to the solution. There is power when two people come together to consummate their marriage. That will surely keep the enemy out. God designed sex to be pleasurable within the bounds of Christian marriage. He intended it to strengthen the bonds of marriage. Once you set the course of your marriage you are living on a spiritual plane covered by the

Ten

blood of Jesus, you will find that the marriage bed will explode with sexual fulfillment.

Questions for You to Reflect On

1. Think about a time when you knew you were spiritually connected to your spouse. What were the circumstances?

2. What are signs that the drift effect has entered your marriage?

3. How can you tell when you're emotionally connected to your spouse? What are the signs?

4. Reflect on a time when your physical connection with your spouse was not what you wanted it to be. What were the circumstances, and what did you do to resolve the issue?

Eleven

Celebrating the Vows

During my grade-school days, I played football on some pretty good teams. We won a lot, and as a child, that can spoil you in playing competitive sports. What I remember the most was the celebrations we had after our wins. Our parents would take us to the nearest pizza place, and we would eat and play video games to our heart's content.

We had so much fun that we began to look forward to the celebrations more than we did the actual games. You see, the celebration made the victory even sweeter. We would sit around and talk about what we did to contribute to the win. We'd go over all the positive aspects of the game. Every now and then, we would discuss the near misses—the situations that could have cost us the game. Then, taking note at Monday's practice, we'd concentrate on what we could do so that the near misses wouldn't happen again.

Similarly, in celebrating our vows, in rejoicing about our victories and critiquing the "near misses" we can help strengthen our marriages. Simply put, it is an action to express gratitude for a blessing God has bestowed on us. We celebrate birthdays, anniversaries, retirements, holidays, sports victories, homecomings, and many other occasions. Absent from this litany of occasions is the celebration of the wedding vow. It is a rare celebratory event when vows are celebrated, even though it was a major promise that was made unto God on the wedding day.

My wife Yolanda and I celebrate our marriage every chance we get. Celebrating simply means taking advantage of the times we have together. We celebrate the unity, the blessing, and the ordination of our marriage by creating new great memories. In celebrating our marriage, we are striving to project a relationship that our children will want to emulate.

Reflecting on your vows will give you the opportunity to share where your marriage has taken you, through the good times and the bad. As you have seen, our beginning wasn't a fairy tale. God's hand had to be in our relationship because everything about our start signaled trouble ahead. Yolanda wasn't ready or even thinking about getting into another relationship, much less getting married, and, at the time, I was not the man she eventually would fall in love with. Our beginning was marked by a struggle of pain, suffering, and heartache. Much to our surprise, they were the ingredients to a recipe that would prepare a great feast of a relationship!

There is no question that the relationship Yolanda and I have would not be as strong as it is, not as spiritually grounded as it is, and not as harmonious for our ministry, had we not experienced the troubles from my addiction, her controlling spirit, and the blending of our families. These experiences taught us how much God loves us and how important it is to keep our vow. This in itself is cause for celebration!

Besides, accepting Christ to be our Lord and Savior and thereby receiving the gift of salvation, our marriage has been the single biggest promise we made in our lifetime. Making such a promise is so important that it must be celebrated. Why would we not want to express our gratitude and appreciation to God for the blessings of our marriage?

You may think: we celebrate our anniversary every year. Why isn't that sufficient? Celebrating anniversaries is different from celebrating your marriage vows. When we consider anniversaries, in most cases, we think of fancy restaurants, luxurious destinations, and special attire to be worn. A celebration of the marriage vows is a spiritual recognition of their importance for a married couple. It is a time when you come together as one to reaffirm the very vows that joined you together, a time for you to recommit to each other and recite the vows you made to each other on your wedding day.

Celebrating your marriage vows gives you the chance as husband and wife to reevaluate and strengthen your marriage by seeing how it honors God. This celebratory time should be a check-in for where you stand in your relationship both with God and your spouse. You both may want to consider where you stood in your spiritual lives on your wedding day to where you stand now in your spiritual lives after several years of being married. Or, you may desire to reflect on what you both have learned about being in love and married to each other through good times and bad. In any event, you have a shared history that is unlike any other couple, a history that is worth reflecting on and celebrating.

Areas that bear reflecting on include how you communicated with each other early in your marriage versus how you communicate with each other now. Or, how you managed your finances then versus how you manage them now. If your relationship is healthy and strong in God, then your marriage will reflect it in all areas. On the other hand, if it is weak, your marriage will reflect that weakness in these same areas.

One thing I know for sure is that on my wedding day my relationship with God was mediocre at best, which led to my marriage becoming mediocre. Today, Yolanda and I have a much stronger and solid relationship with God, which has led to a stronger and more thriving marriage. As we stop to celebrate our vows, we can see the importance of a relationship with God and how it must be our foundation of our marriage.

Fan the Flame to Keep It Burning

Rekindling your vows will help to reignite the places in your marriage where the flame has gone out. Why has it blown out? Taking each other for granted is one reason that may have caused it to go out. For instance, neglecting to tell your spouse that you love him or her, or failing to spend time together by going on dates, are ways that a spouse may be taken for granted.

No matter how your relationship started off, God was there in the mix! He was the One who ignited the fire in you as a couple! It is now the job of both of you to keep that fire going as expressed so appropriately in LEVITICUS 6:13:

I Thee Wed

*Remember, the fire must be kept burning on
the altar at all times. It must never go out.*

You can help to fan the flames in your marriage by
pondering these questions:

- What makes your relationship invaluable to
  you?
- What makes you cherish what you have?

Because God lit the initial fire in you, whatever is
needed to rekindle it, already lies within in each of you.

When I was in the army, I really missed my daughters.
While spending time away from them, I would think about
those times when we were together when I failed to spend
quality time with them. My time away from them forced
me to reflect on those missed opportunities, and much of
my quiet time was spent thinking about how I would make
it up to them.

In marriage, we often wait for periods of separation to
force us to think about how we can rekindle our
relationships by spending quality time together. The
marriage flame must be fanned so that it can burn at its
brightest and hottest. With God's help, you can re-ignite
the flame in your marriage so that it burns as brightly as on
the day of your wedding. All you need do is go to Him in
prayer. Ask for wisdom, knowledge and understanding to
be the spouse that He has called you to be.

No doubt, you have heard the saying "people make time
for things that matter and are important to them." We must
do away with the excuse that we don't have time to

celebrate our vows. Yes, life is busy, and the world pulls at us in many different ways. But you can't be a good mother or father if you are not first a good wife and husband, and you can't be a good wife and husband if you are not a good follower of Christ. One affects the other if they are not in proper order.

Here's how you can now prioritize celebrating your vows and how you can think of it as an appointment that you can't miss—a time to celebrate your commitment both to God and to your spouse:

Plan a ceremony to renew your vows.

A vow renewal ceremony is a way to celebrate your marriage and to reaffirm your commitment to God and each other. No matter how long you have been married, renewing your vows can be a surefire way to remember and honor the promise.

To enhance the ceremony, consider posting your vows on an easel for all to read. Ask attendees to sign them around the borders as a remembrance of witnessing the ceremony. Afterwards, display the easel on a prominent wall in your home. Every few years move it to a different visible location to keep it front of mind.

Have a vow victory celebration.

This is a time for married couples to meet and reflect on the meaning of their vows. Each attendee should bring the most meaningful parts of his or her vows to the celebration for everyone to see. Each couple should share a testimony of what the vow has meant to them in their marriage. This celebration might be hosted every five to ten years to commemorate the marriage commitment of couples. These five statements can inspire and help motivate you to celebrate your vows:

- God is worth celebrating.
- Don't celebrate your vows alone.
- It's not ordinary to celebrate your marriage vows; it's extraordinary.
- You can afford to celebrate.
- Celebration is not a selfish act.

Consider what Paul says about love as you celebrate your commitment to each other through holy matrimony:

> *Don't just pretend to love others. Really love them. Hate what is wrong. Hold tightly to what is good. Love each other with genuine affection, and take delight in honoring each other. Never be lazy, but work hard and serve the Lord enthusiastically. Rejoice in our confident hope. Be patient in trouble, and keep on praying. When God's people are in need, be ready to help them. Always be eager to practice hospitality.*
> — ROMANS 12: 9–13

In this scripture, Paul is teaching how we should live out our faith every day as followers of Christ now that we are one and are on this journey together. As married couples, we have a responsibility to keep our love and our promises to God alive. Here are some suggestions that will support you in this charge, as well as keep the fire of love burning throughout your marriage.

Serve one another.

Each day determine what you can do to serve your spouse. Do something that speaks to his or her heart and lift your spouse's spirits immediately.

Practice spiritual hospitality.

Be hospitable to those seeking to marry or who are newly married. Spiritual hospitality is listening actively and being available to your spouse for encouragement and to share your insights.

Share your testimony of faith.

Share your testimony to other couples who are following you on your journey. Opportunities for you to speak up and speak out in love, relationships, and marriage will present themselves to you. Don't miss this open door. Extend your heart to them.

Train your children.

There is no better way to show God's love and your commitment than for children to see it lived out in their home or family. Children respond to what you do more than what you say.

Don't settle for mediocrity.

Do not conform to the patterns of the world. As married

couples devoted to God, you are new creatures in Christ. Resist the worldly focus on fame, fortune, and material possessions. Don't give in to gossip or slander.

Continue bearing the fruits of the spirit.
The fruits of the Spirit are love, joy, peace, patience, kindness, goodness, faith, gentleness, and self-control. This is who you are and how you should live; it is how you should respond to life when it throws you a curve ball.

Stay empty before the Lord.
Surrender unto the Lord the things of this world that He has entrusted to you. This entails your home, ambitions, achievements, finances and ministry. By doing so, God will use them to bless others and to send assignments through you so that He may be glorified.

Questions for You to Reflect On

1. When was the last time you attended a couple's celebration of their wedding vows? How did it make you feel?

2. How has the flame dimmed in your relationship? What do you think you can do to reignite it?

3. What do you cherish most about your relationship?

4. What couple or couples can you identify to jointly celebrate your vows? Would you be open to reaching out to them to do so?

Twelve

Sources of Support
for Keeping the Vows

Along your marriage journey, you will need all the support you can get to keep your marriage intact and focused on the union God intended by bringing the two of you together. To this end, there are several resources available for married couples to consider.

Since the founding of our marriage ministry, Live in Peace Ministries, LLC, Billy and I have worked with couples individually and in group settings to help them remain committed to their vows. In doing so, we came to find that some couples profit most from spending private time with us whether in person or via Skype video conferencing, while others prefer being part of a group setting. In any case, we have found it to be critical to link up with other godly couples who can walk alongside you during your marriage journey. This recommendation is not only for newlyweds or those couples whose marriage has reached a stage where the flame has burnt out. We firmly believe that every couple should have a safe harbor in which to grow together as a couple and to learn how to be and to stay married. In our experience, this can be achieved in four ways, depending on what stage you are in your marriage: through a marriage mentor, a marriage coach, a marriage counselor, and a marriage retreat/conference.

Marriage Mentors

Marriage mentors are a great resource for married couples, whether a couple is newly married or has been married for several years. It is a comfort to have someone accessible to you who can lend a listening ear and help you to navigate the sometimes choppy waters of marriage. A reliable source of support and encouragement, a marriage mentor can be turned to for a specific reason, for a season, or for a lifetime.

A marriage mentor is not someone who claims to know it all about the challenges of being in a committed relationship. It is someone who has journeyed down the path you are beginning to tread and who may be farther down the road than you. Such a person will be objective toward you and your marriage and not take sides in disagreements, but will give you the whole truth and lead you back to Jesus when you go astray.

In order to find such a person, you can start by investigating your church. After all, many congregations now have marriage mentoring programs or support groups for married couples where you might find Christian couples whose values toward holy matrimony closely align with yours.

Another option is to consider a married couple that you know whom you admire. Perhaps you have been made aware of details of their marriage journey through their own testimony or through others, and you admire how they managed to overcome a difficult test to their union. This very couple could well serve as your marriage mentor. On the other hand, while not privy to the intimate details of their marriage, perhaps you have identified a couple who, by the way they relate to each other publicly, embody the very values that a godly marriage requires.

You might think, "But I don't know them personally." While such hesitation is understandable, you can't afford not to extend yourself to introduce yourselves to them. They will likely be honored and humbled to have been sought out by someone who has observed the way they relate to each other in marriage and have singled them out as a couple to be emulated. To break the ice, you might compliment them on how they carry themselves as a married couple and invite them to coffee to learn what the ingredient to such a visibly blessed union is. It is very likely that they will be surprised by the compliment and be more than willing to share their wisdom on such a topic, which it is unlikely that anyone has broached with them before.

It is a blessing to have another married couple available to turn to when you can't seem to get along with your spouse or when you're unsure why your spouse has taken the passive aggressive approach of giving you the silent treatment. You will find that this support will be one of the most important preventive strategies that you can employ to rescue your marriage and to make sure it is thriving.

We strongly encourage you not to seek out your parents for this role. Although they may have the benefit of having been in a long marriage, the closeness of family ties prevents them from being truly objective, a situation that can create a wedge between you and your spouse during a time of marital difficulty between the two of you. Nor should your mentor be a close friend, for the same reason. Someone married who has experience or training in mentoring married couples and who is willing to share his or her personal testimony from a godly perspective is the ideal person for this role.

Marriage Coaches

A marriage coach is a trained and certified individual or couple who helps married couples overcome obstacles to a loving, God-centered marriage. In doing so, they offer advice that can help a couple resolve conflicts that arise in the marriage. Marriage coaches have helped many couples repair and sustain their marriages so that they can survive and, ultimately, thrive. According to PROVERBS 12:15:

> *Fools think their own way is right, but the wise listen to others.*

A marriage coach will listen to both sides of the story, gather all the necessary facts, respond with questions specific to your situation, and then advise a course of action designed to remedy the problem. Such a coach will help you identify where the marriage currently stands and help you clear the path to where you both would like it to be.

Taking personal accountability for your role in the breakdown is a ground rule for working with a marriage coach. You can choose to meet with a coach once a week or once a month for an agreed upon length of time.

Twelve

Typically, during each meeting, you will be given instructions and homework to work on for the next meeting. Each session usually opens with a recap of the previous meeting and the progress that you feel you have achieved toward your goal since that meeting.

Couples should be prepared to take notes at these meetings. They also must be mindful that it is they who are doing the work on their marriage and not the coach. This is a key requirement for your success working with a coach. The primary responsibility of a coach is to guide you through the steps that you both have determined to take to improve your marriage.

It cannot be emphasized enough that working with a marriage coach is heavily dependent on the two of you and the amount of effort you are willing to expend to resolve the issues that have beset your marriage.

Billy and I truly love working with couples who have chosen to take advantage of the services of a marriage coach. Recently, we worked with a couple who had been married for a few years and had just transitioned to life in a new town. Their goal was to learn how to communicate with each other better and to minimize the situations where their disagreements inevitably led to arguments.

After they shared their concerns, it became clear that the wife didn't trust her husband, and allowed him no room for error. To make matters worse, they did not agree on the boundaries she had placed on him—boundaries that had never come up for discussion. Later, when the wife attempted to hold the husband accountable for a certain action, he would become upset, failing to understand why she held him to something that he believed was unimportant. As their coaches, Billy and I walked them through the various levels of communication in a marriage and how to achieve the level of vulnerability and trust.

Once they understood how to talk to each other, they began to hear what each one had to say. They soon realized that the problem wasn't just one of communication, although that was how the problem was being manifested in the marriage, its root was the lack of trust in their marriage. The only way they realized this was by responding to the leading questions we had asked them during our sessions. This is the benefit—and blessing—of working with a marriage coach. He or she will reveal to you, in a nonjudgmental way, all that you have shared with them, enabling you to evaluate it dispassionately and determine the best course of action.

Pastoral Counselors

Pastoral counselors bring to their qualifications the added dimension of rootedness in the Christian faith in helping couples solve their marital problems. God is at the center of their recommendations in solving marriage problems and is always the focal point of the counseling session. The methodology used during counseling with a pastoral counselor will rest heavily on your belief in God and Jesus Christ, along with your faith in God's Word. Prayer is the centerpiece of this form of marital remediation.

For instance, a remedy may involve reading scripture as opposed to reading a book or passage relating to your particular marriage issue. A great benefit to working with a pastoral counselor is that often it comes at no financial cost to you and your spouse as you address issues that impact your marriage. This is opposed to seeing a marriage therapist, who charges an hourly rate for his or her services.

You may find that a pastor, before he or she agrees to counsel you, will first ascertain the level of your faith life before listening to your concerns about your marriage. He or she will then help you to confront the issue you are experiencing and apply scripture to the situation when trying to resolve it. Not only will a pastoral counselor apply a scriptural interpretation to resolving the conflict, he or she will seek its correction through prayer. In this way, pastors support the institution of marriage among the flock over which they preside, and they do so in strictest confidentiality. In doing so, they can leave you with the sense of hope and encouragement that you can maintain your commitment to your marriage, while at the same time reminding you of the promises you made to each other before God.

For the both of us, seeking out your pastor for counseling is a first priority that we strongly encourage. After all, your pastor is your shepherd, and it is his or her responsibility to watch over their sheep. For obvious reasons stated earlier, the only exception to seeking out your pastor for counseling is if the pastor is your parent or close relative. Otherwise, such a counselor will surely cover you with prayer and comfort in a spiritually fulfilling way.

Licensed Professional Counselors

Marriage counselors are licensed therapists or ordained ministers trained in the area of marriage counseling. As licensed professionals, they are required to have professional training in human psychology and the related behavioral and social sciences.

Licensed professional counselors help couples understand how their pasts may have contributed to issues that affect the marriage today. In an objective and nonjudgmental way, they listen to each party in the marriage to help guide them to a solution. Although a minority of these professionals also have pastoral training, indicated by the degreed designation after their names, the great majority of them are mandated not to use any form of biblical influence during their counseling services. These professionals typically do not pray for you or refer you to scripture for resolution or direction; nor do they seek out the Holy Spirit to direct them in helping you resolve a specific marital issue. Their services can be very beneficial to troubled marriages that are headed toward dissolution and are well worth the financial investment if you find that the wounds of your past are so deep that they will need a more trained psychological evaluation.

In this instance, seeking out a licensed professional counselor would absolutely be the best choice. There are some areas of the human psyche that have caused us to behave in ways that we do not always understand. Under these circumstances, seeing a licensed professional counselor will be the best recommendation, as they have the capability of helping you to arrive at a long-term

solution for your specific needs. Indeed, as expressed in
PROVERBS 19:20:

> *Get all the advice and instruction you can, so*
> *you will be wise the rest of your life.*

Marriage Retreat/Conference

A marriage retreat or conference is designed as a weekend
or week-long getaway just for the two of you. They are
normally held at a retreat center or hotel. These events offer
the opportunity to relax, reflect, and renew your marriage.
There are retreats that are specific to the condition of your
marriage and others that are more general for the marriage
population. During this time away, you are able to learn
from marriage experts as they share their life lessons, tips,
and strategies to keep your marriage strong. There is also
ample time for you and your spouse to be alone to be
present with one another without distractions.

Over the last couple of years, Billy and I have attended
a minimum of two retreats per year just to focus on the
state of our marriage. We also host an annual retreat and
conference for couples to attend. We believe that time away
from the hustle and bustle of your daily routine gives you
the room to focus on the needs of your spouse. It is like a
reset button you can push each year. Every married couple
should attend a retreat once a year or at least once every
other year. It is a key ingredient to living happily ever after.

Online Marriage Courses

Outside of the weekend getaway retreats/conferences
there are numerous opportunities to take marriage courses

online. This platform gives you the opportunity to learn and grow in the comfort of your home. We find that participating in ongoing classes is a more cost effective way to enrich your marriage. Some of the training you can find is free, while others require a minimal investment. You can connect with the leading marriage experts and other couples in a group setting, and the opportunity to learn from each other while being guided by the instructor is priceless. We highly recommend this option for couples if one party doesn't want a getaway experience or if financial resources are limited. To learn more about courses hosted by Live in Peace Ministries, LLC, visit our website for the latest class listings (www.liveinpeaceministries.org).

There are many resources available for you for finding such a professional. First, you can ask your medical doctor for recommendations. They normally have a list of doctors they are comfortable referring to you. You can also visit the American Association of Marriage and Family Therapy (www.aamft.org) for therapists in your area. Finally, you can do a full search on Google under the subject "marriage therapists in my area." It will provide numerous sites for you to review.

No matter what your marriage needs now, we want you to know that God is the only One who can heal and restore it. Even though you might be experiencing the best season that you think is possible in your marriage, God will show you how to sustain it and ensure that it continues to thrive.

In the spirit of encouragement for your marriage, whether you are veterans of marriage, newly married, or contemplating marriage, we urge you to make a decision today. We recommend that you meditate on PROVERBS 15:22 and MATTHEW 6:33:

Plans go wrong for lack of advice;
many advisers bring success.

Seek the Kingdom of God above all else, and
live righteously, and he will give you
everything you need.

What is everything? The things you have been longing for and believing in God to do for your marriage. He is willing, ready, and able to bless your union. All you have to do is take the first step and trust in Him. The same God who laid His loving and healing hand on us is the same God that has His hand open and ready to receive you and your spouse. The same God who sent His only son Jesus Christ to suffer and die for our sins and raised Him from the dead so that we may be free. He's the same God who has already won for you the battle for your marriage. It's time to make Him your priority and your marriage comes right after that relationship. All you have to do is surrender to Him, and He will do the rest.

Questions for You to Reflect On

1. Are there marriage mentors who you can identify to help you along your marriage path? Who might they be?

2. Do you think marriage coaches should be consulted during a marriage crisis, or before

one develops in a marriage? Why or why not?

3. Why might many couples be disinclined to seek the services of a marriage counselor when their marriage is in trouble? Do you agree with their point of view? Why or why not?

Postscript

Our Prayer for Your Marriage

Lord, we pray, that you would draw these, your people, who are readers of this book into a more personal relationship with you. We pray that you would restore the broken pieces for those who are hurting and struggling in their marriage. We pray, Lord God, that you would destroy the grip that addiction, complacency, materialism, control, stubbornness or selfishness has on their lives. Release your power in Jesus's name and destroy that grip. Teach all married couples to depend on You, God, as their Source, rather than their own resources.

We pray Lord God, that you will reveal yourself to them in a mighty way—in a way that they have never even imagined. We pray Lord God, that you would order their steps and give them the wisdom and the discernment they need to make the right choices in their marriage. We pray Lord God, that you would be a bridge of grace and mercy over troubled waters in their marriage, that you would direct their paths as they begin to trust you even more in their marriage.

Lord, your Word teaches us that there is power of life and death in our tongue. We give you total control over our words, both spoken and unspoken. We pray, Lord God, that you would send a refreshing spirit of love, joy, peace, patience, kindness, goodness, faithfulness, gentleness, and self-control upon the lives of all married couples. Help them, God, not to become disenchanted or build resentment toward one another. Help them to extend grace to their spouses, which has been freely given unto them by you, our Lord and Savior Jesus Christ. Surround them with wise counsel in the form of godly married couples, pastoral leaders, and marriage counselors who will cover them and pray for and with them along the way.

We pray Lord God, that you would release a spirit of discernment upon those who are not yet married but have this desire upon their hearts. We ask God that you would comfort them in times of loneliness and remind them of how much you love them. We pray, Lord God, that when they are led to temptation, that you would strengthen them and not allow their foot to slip. We pray that they would honor you with their bodies in their waiting season. Help them to see, Lord God, the plan and purpose that You have for their lives, and may they grow to understand that You never sleep nor slumber.

We ask these prayers while giving you the praise, glory, and honor. In your Son Jesus Christ's precious name, Amen.

About the Authors

Live in Peace Ministries, LLC was founded by Billy and Yolanda Jackson. These two are a force to be reckoned with when it comes to "real life" marriage and family situations. Two very different souls from broken first marriages found God's true love the second time around in 2004 and blended their families together through marriage in 2007. They now have four beautiful children and three adorable grandchildren.

Billy is no stranger to serving others. He is an army veteran and has served the Nashville, Tennessee, community in law enforcement with the Metropolitan Police Department for seventeen years. While continuing his service with the government, he has stepped deeper into his calling as a minister of the Gospel and has a deep passion for strengthening marriages.

Yolanda's passion to serve others started in the beauty-wellness industry where she served in leadership for eighteen years. Stepping out on faith, she transitioned from Corporate America in 2014 to serve as the Director of Spiritual Development for Olive Branch Church, where she instituted bible study small groups and oversaw all youth and teen initiatives. In October 2016, Yolanda began her full-time service with Live in Peace Ministries, LLC.

The ministry's mission is to know and love God, to become the best we can be, and to go out and equip others to do the same.

Billy and Yolanda are fully committed to teaching married people that life is better together, inspiring them to believe that no matter where the broken pieces have fallen, they still can live in peace with God. With this hope, they passionately empower married people to live relentlessly as examples of the Gospel for their family, friends, community, and those they will encounter along the path God has laid out for them.

Live in Peace Ministries is a Christian-based organization that stands on God's Word for the truth, and it is the truth that will set you free.

www.liveinpeaceministries.org

Notes